Email us at

schoolhome.kids@gmail.com

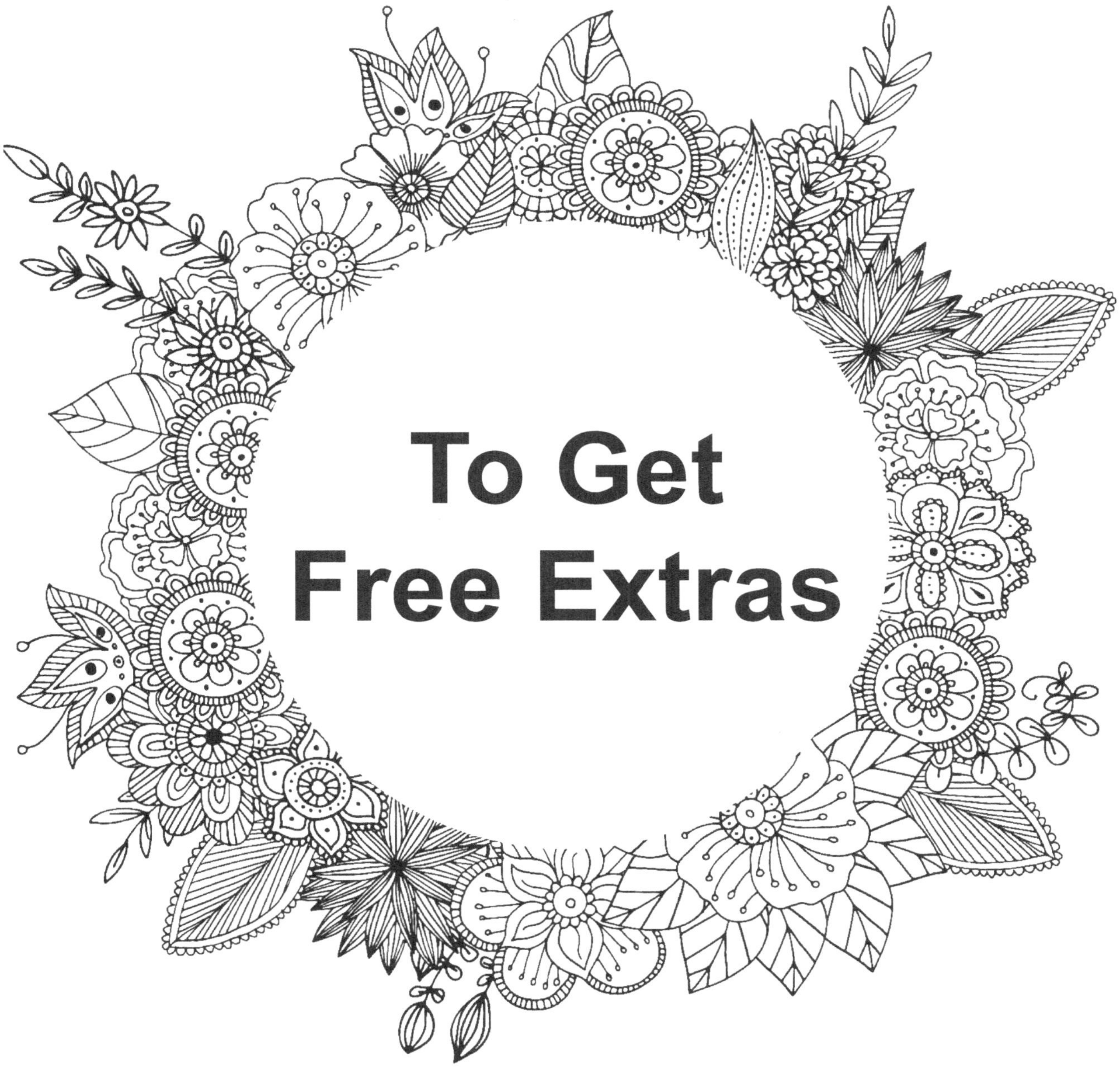

To Get
Free Extras

just titre the email

- Adult Coloring Book-

And we will send some extra
surprises your way !.

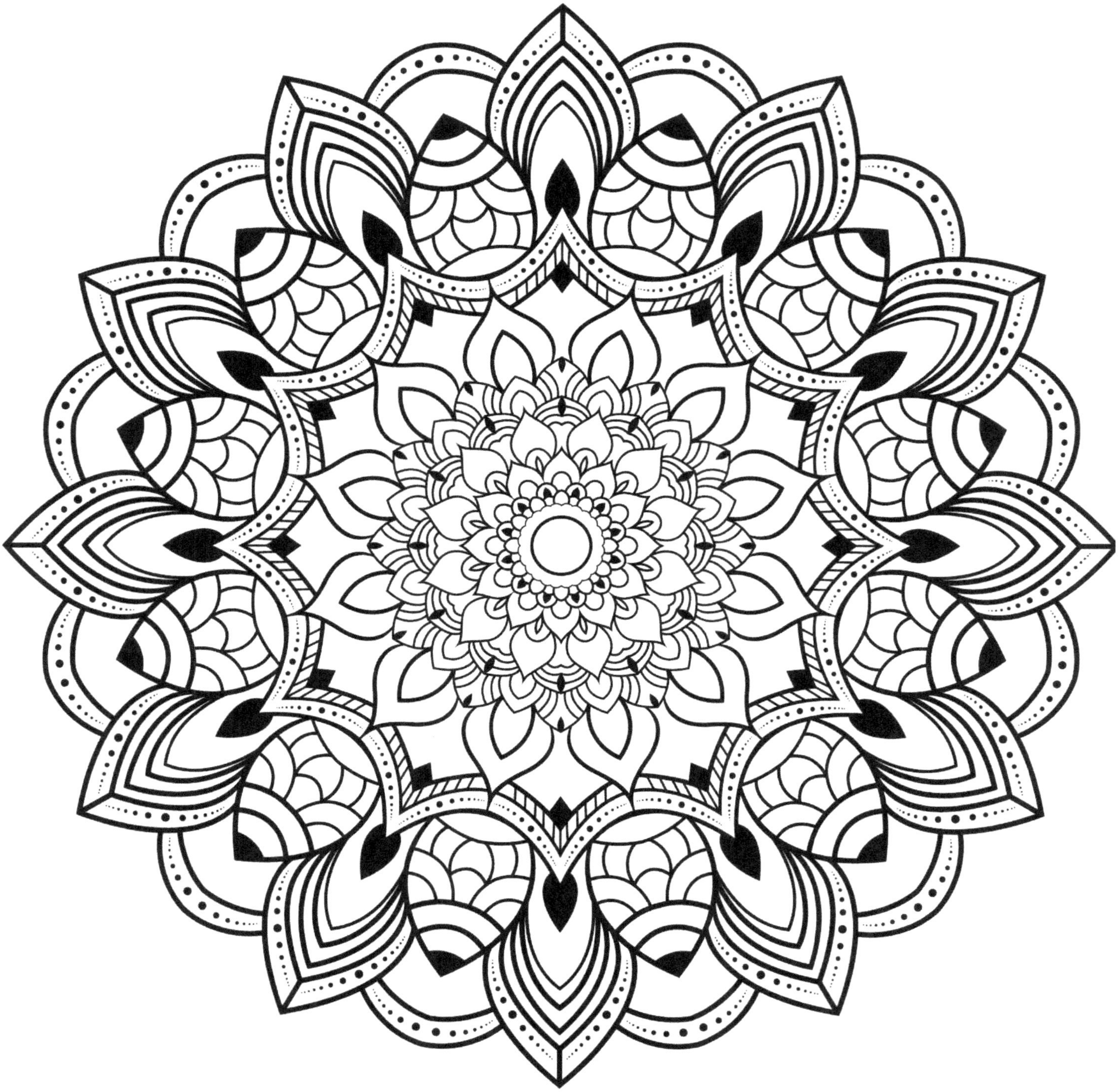

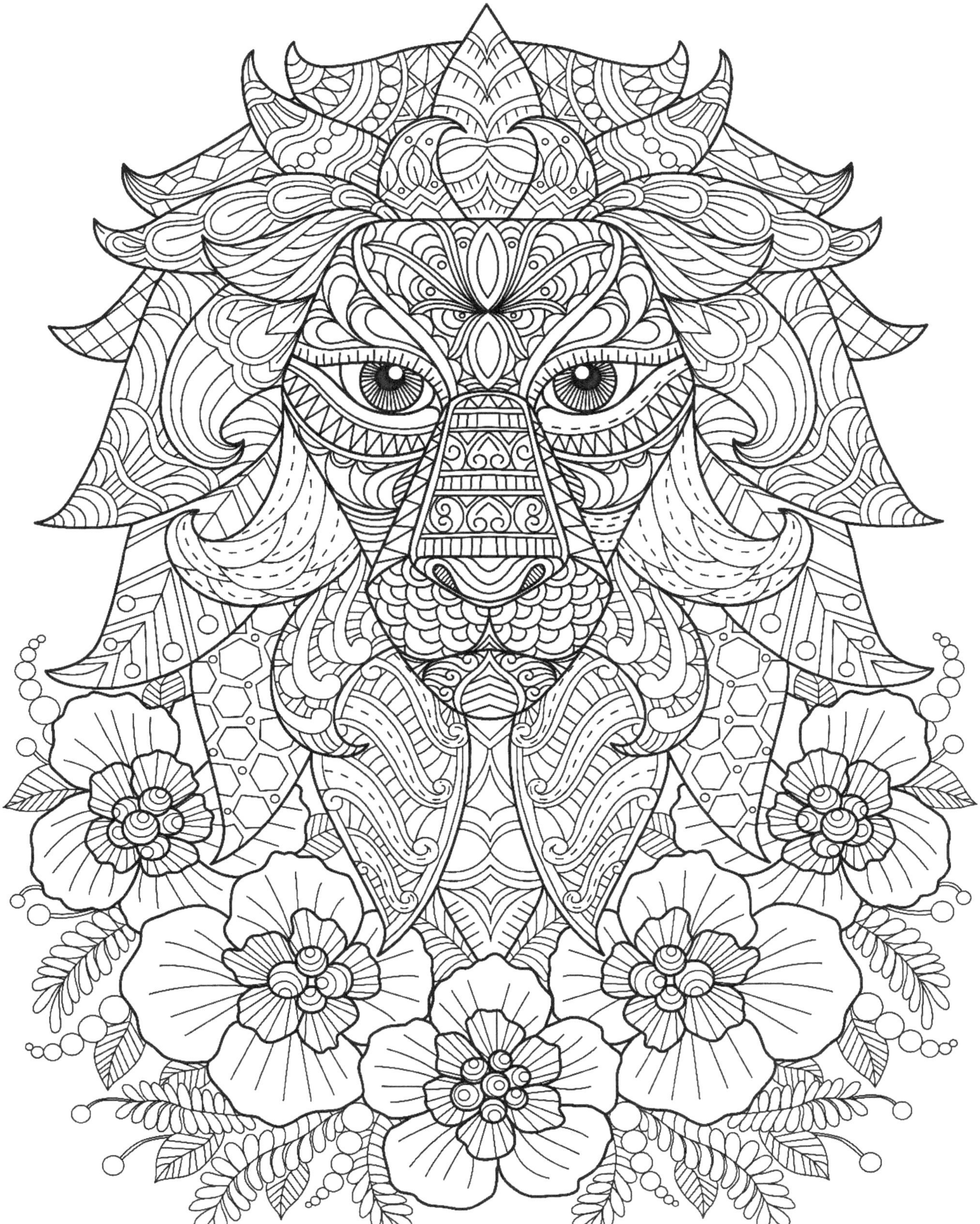

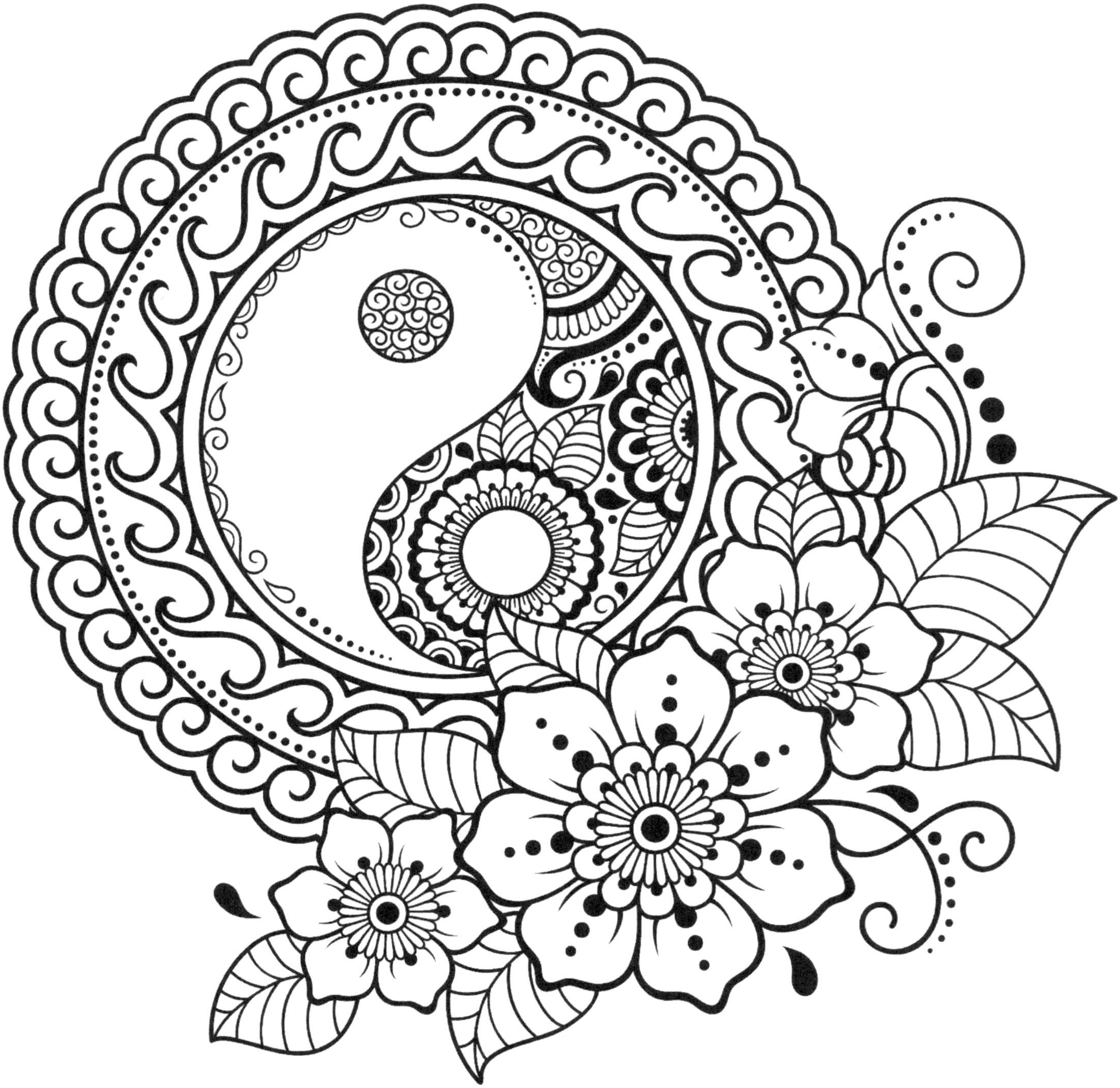

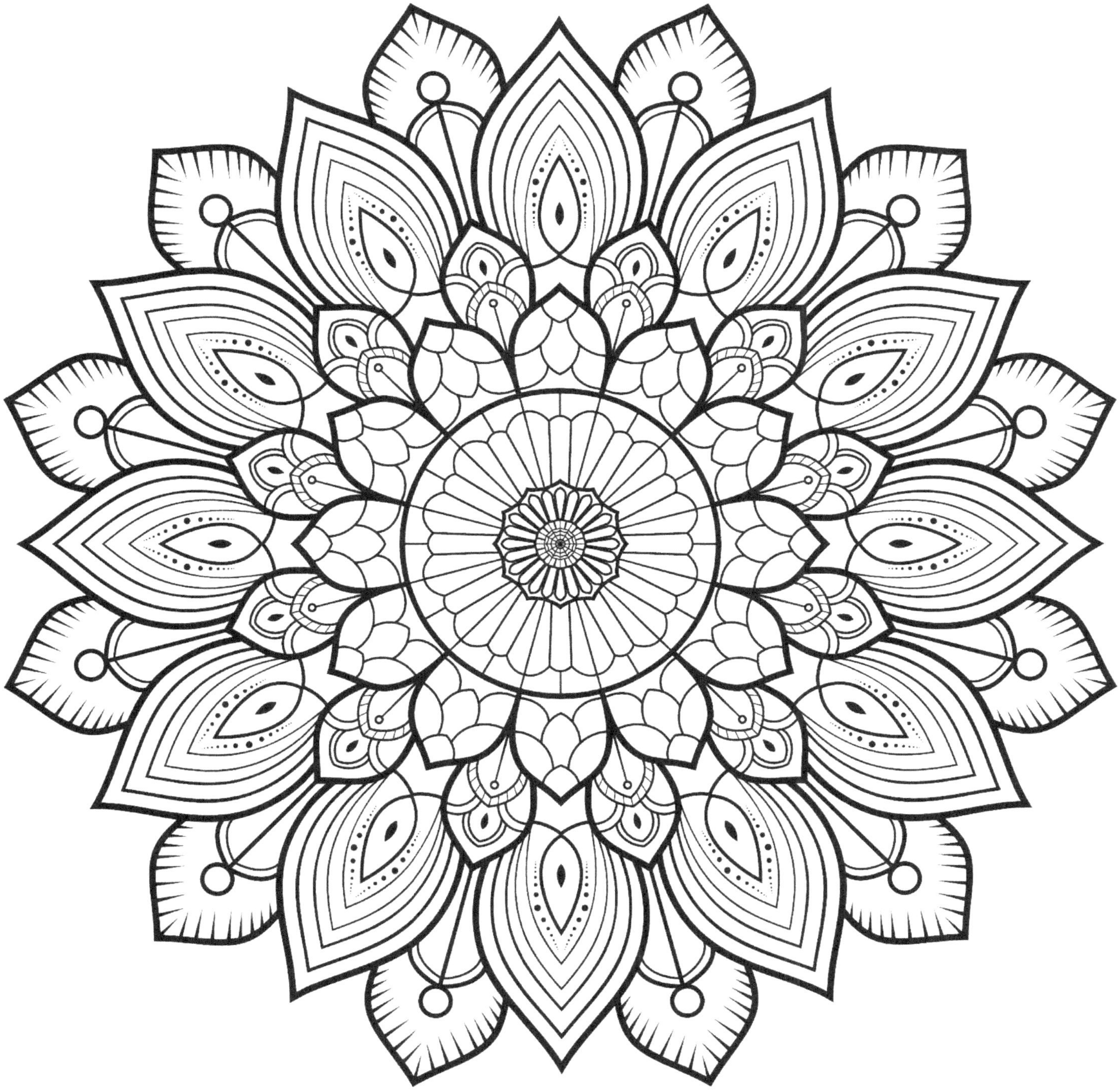

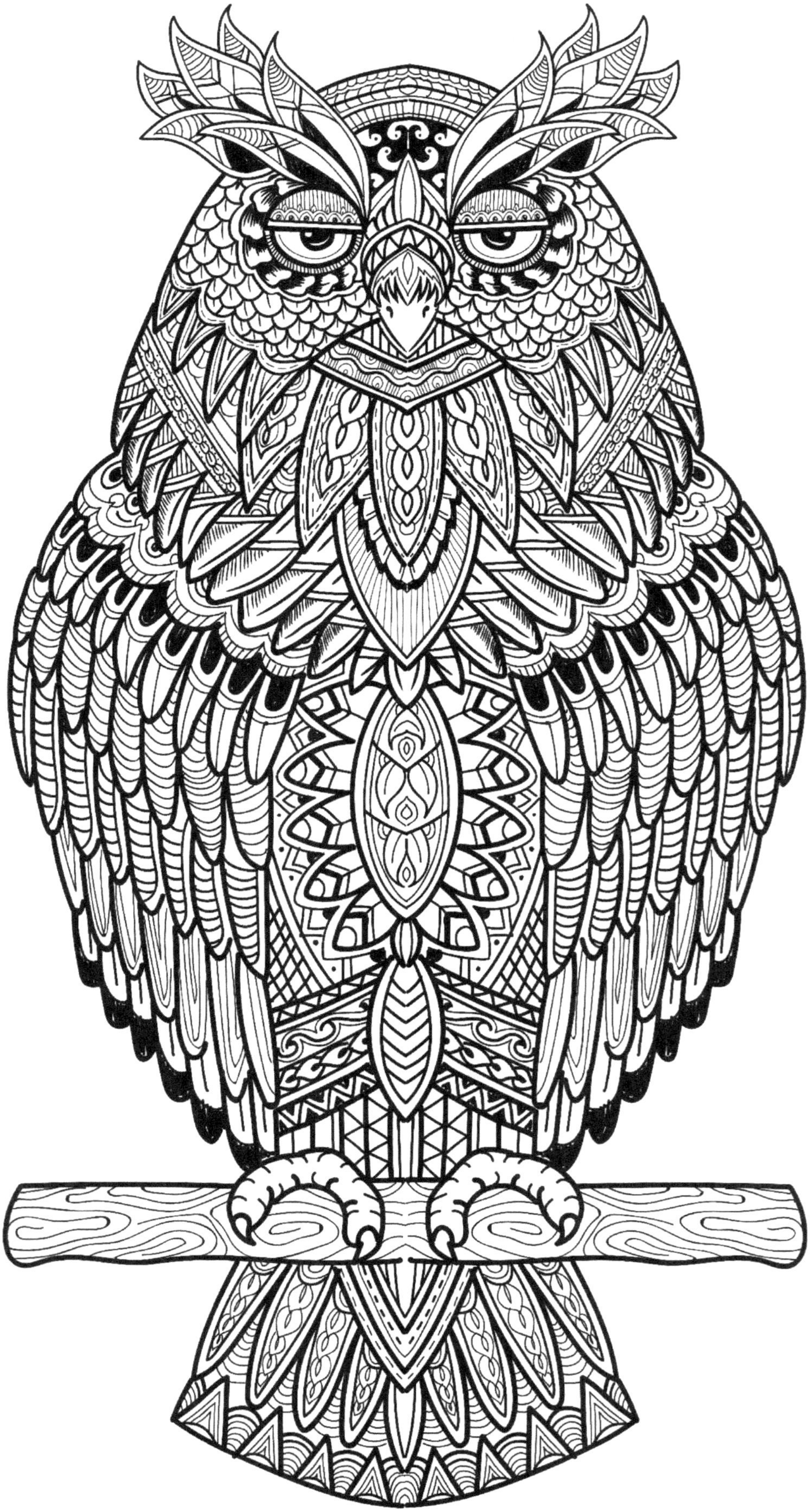

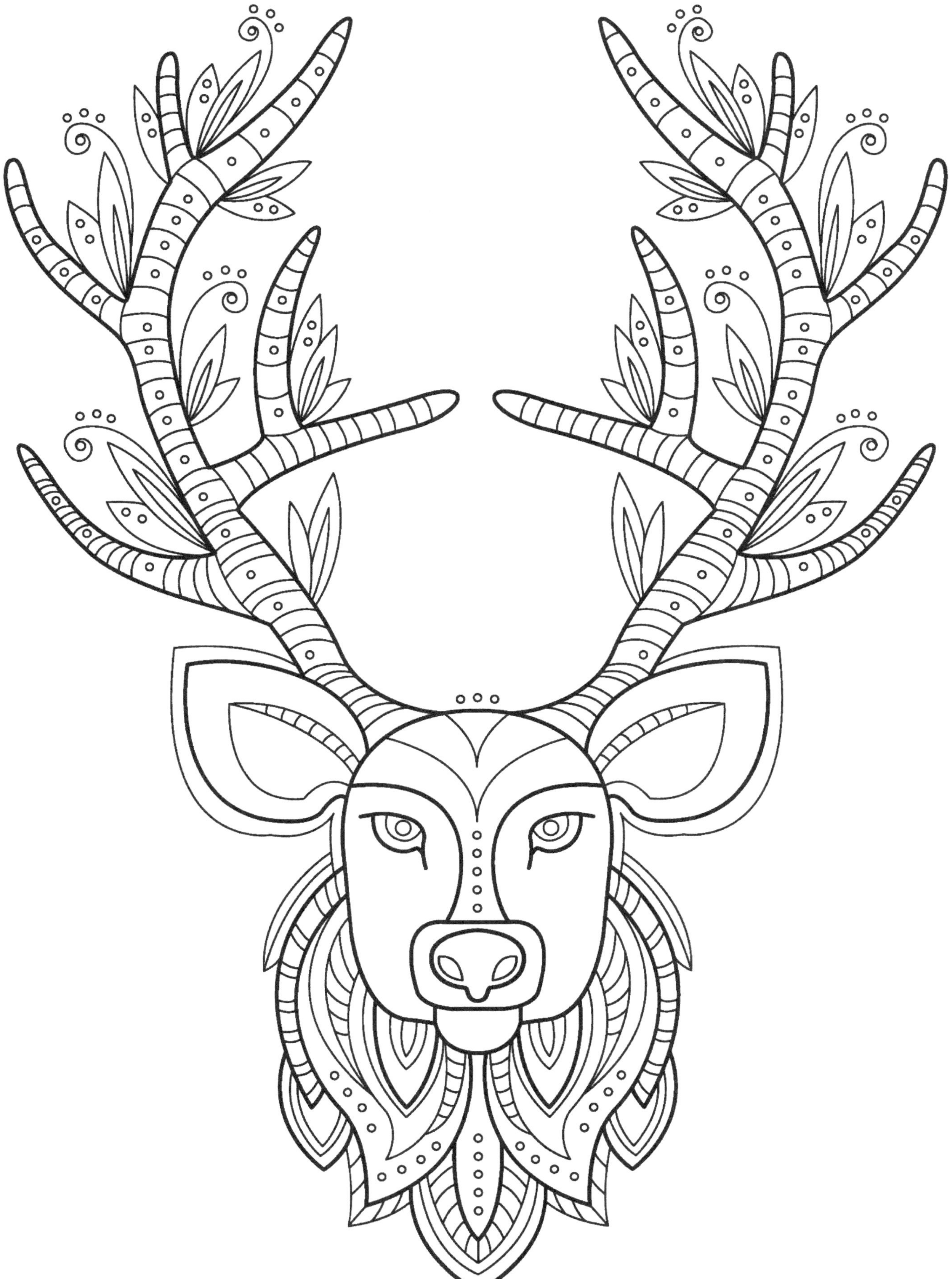

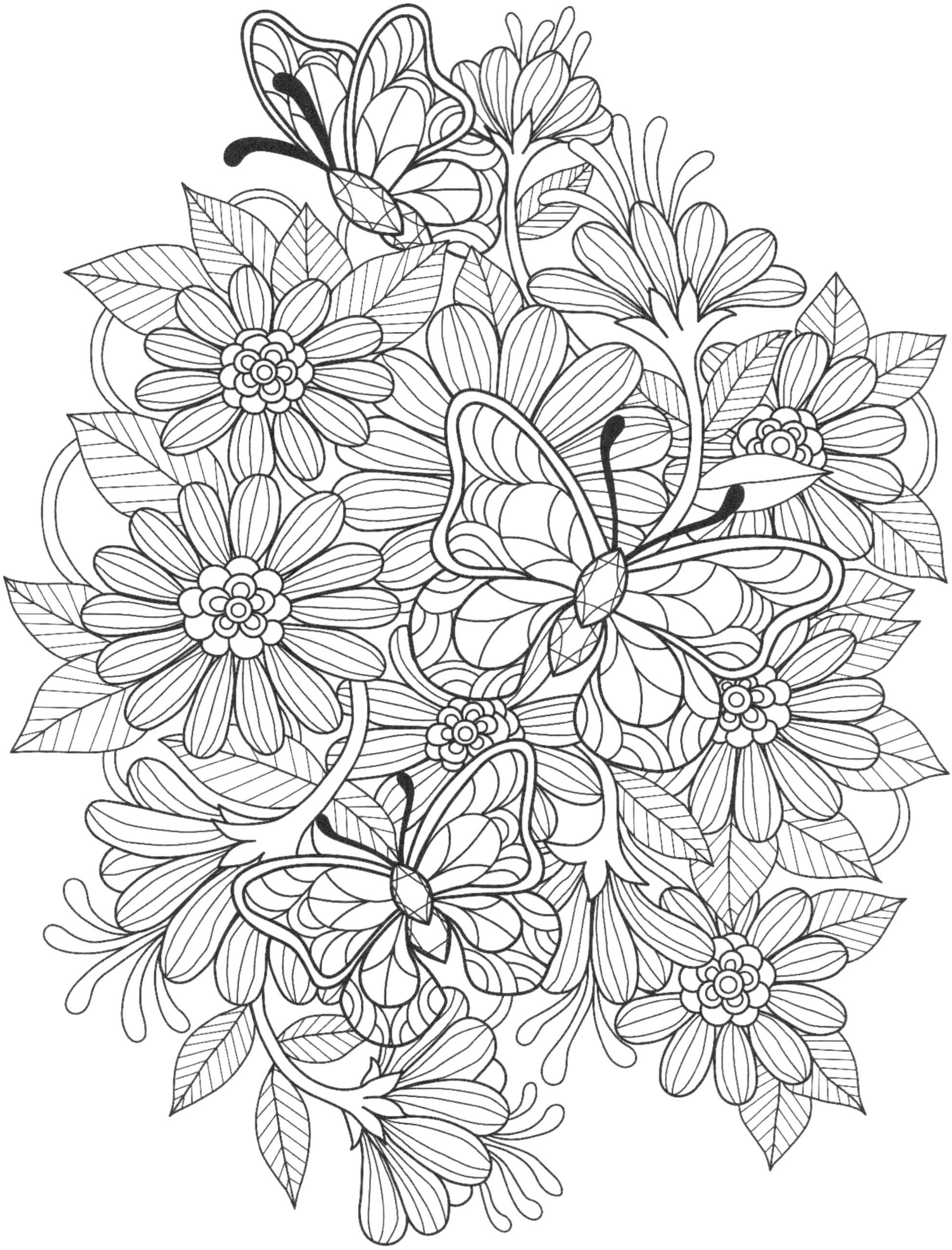

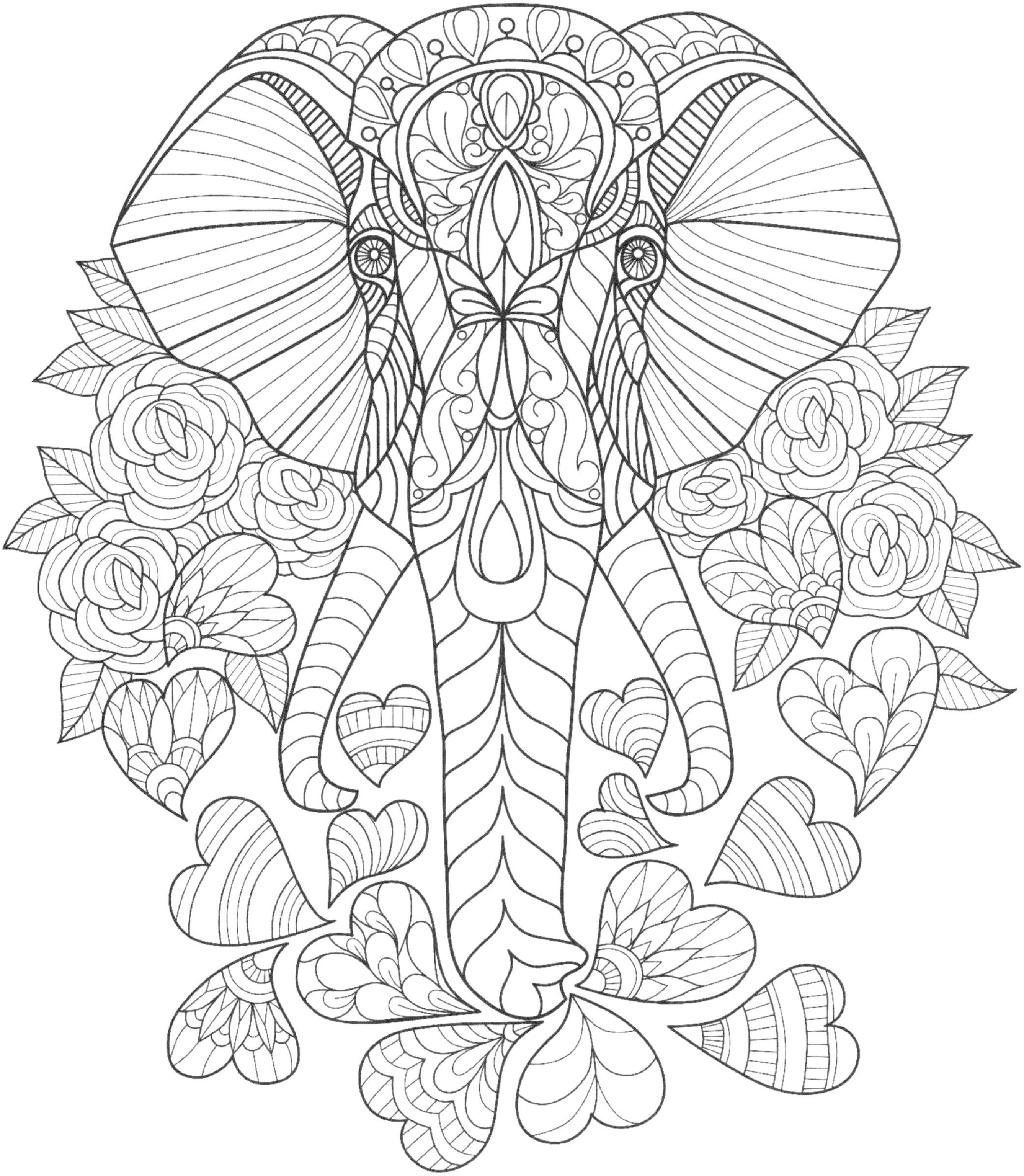

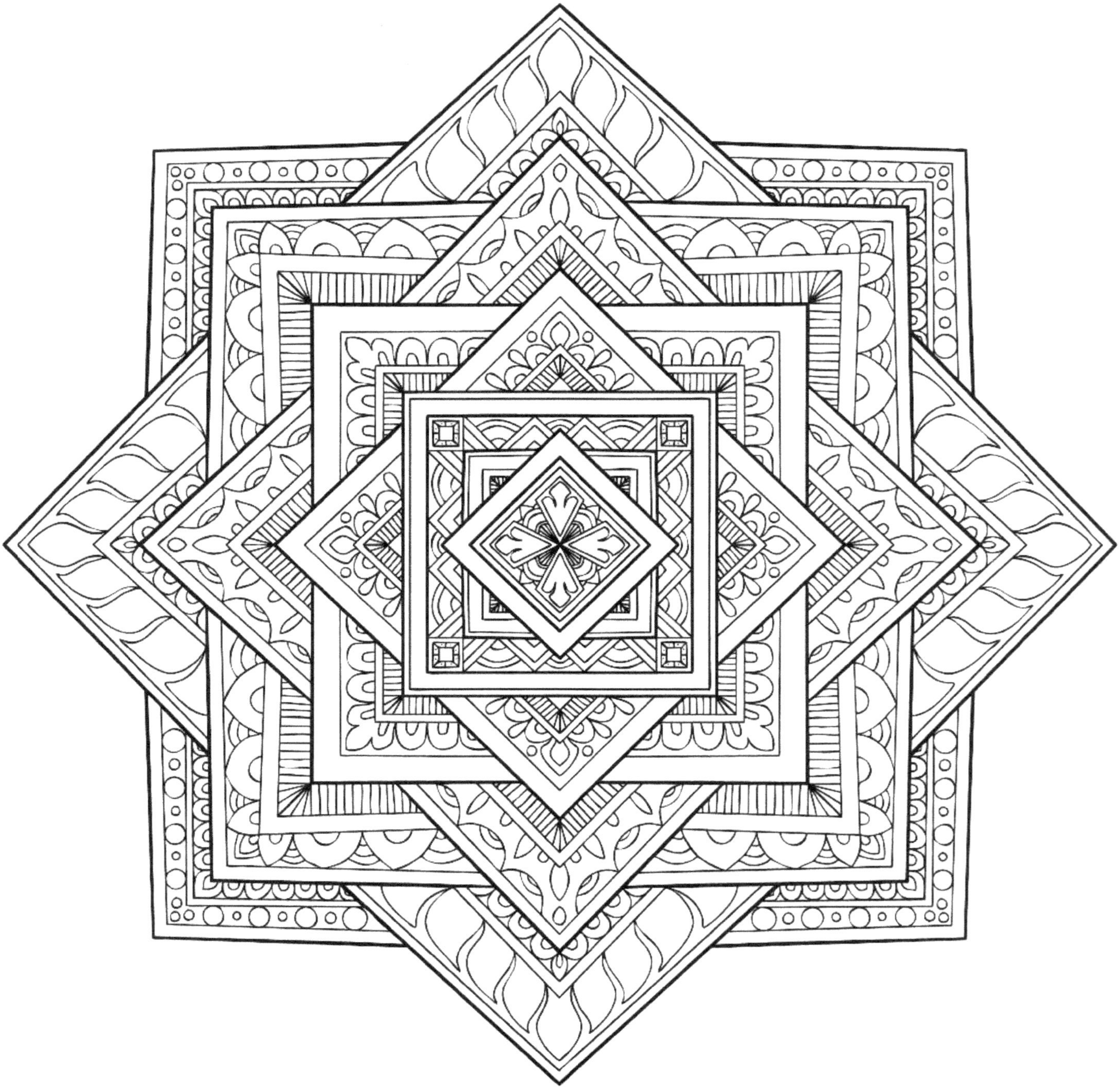

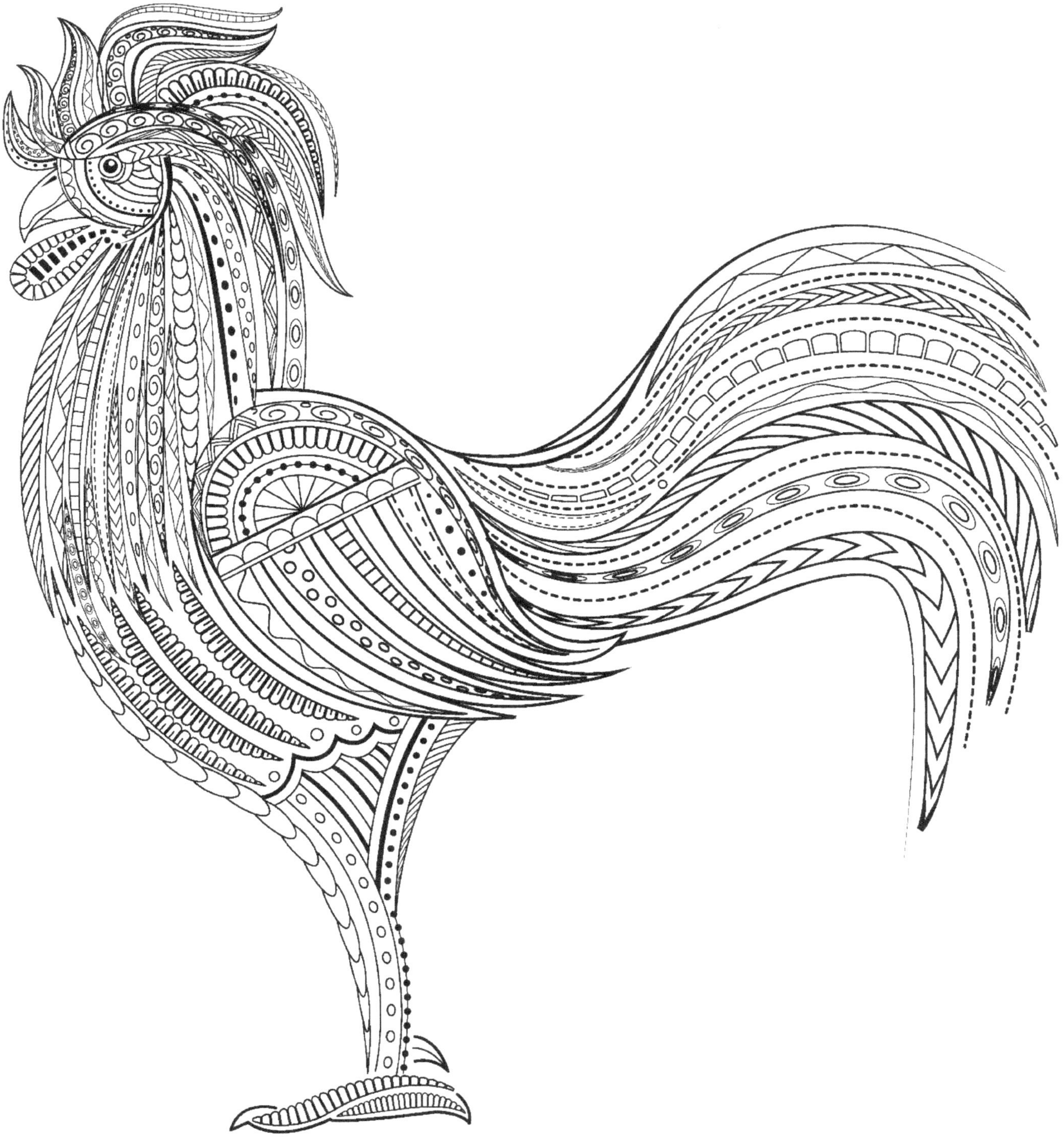

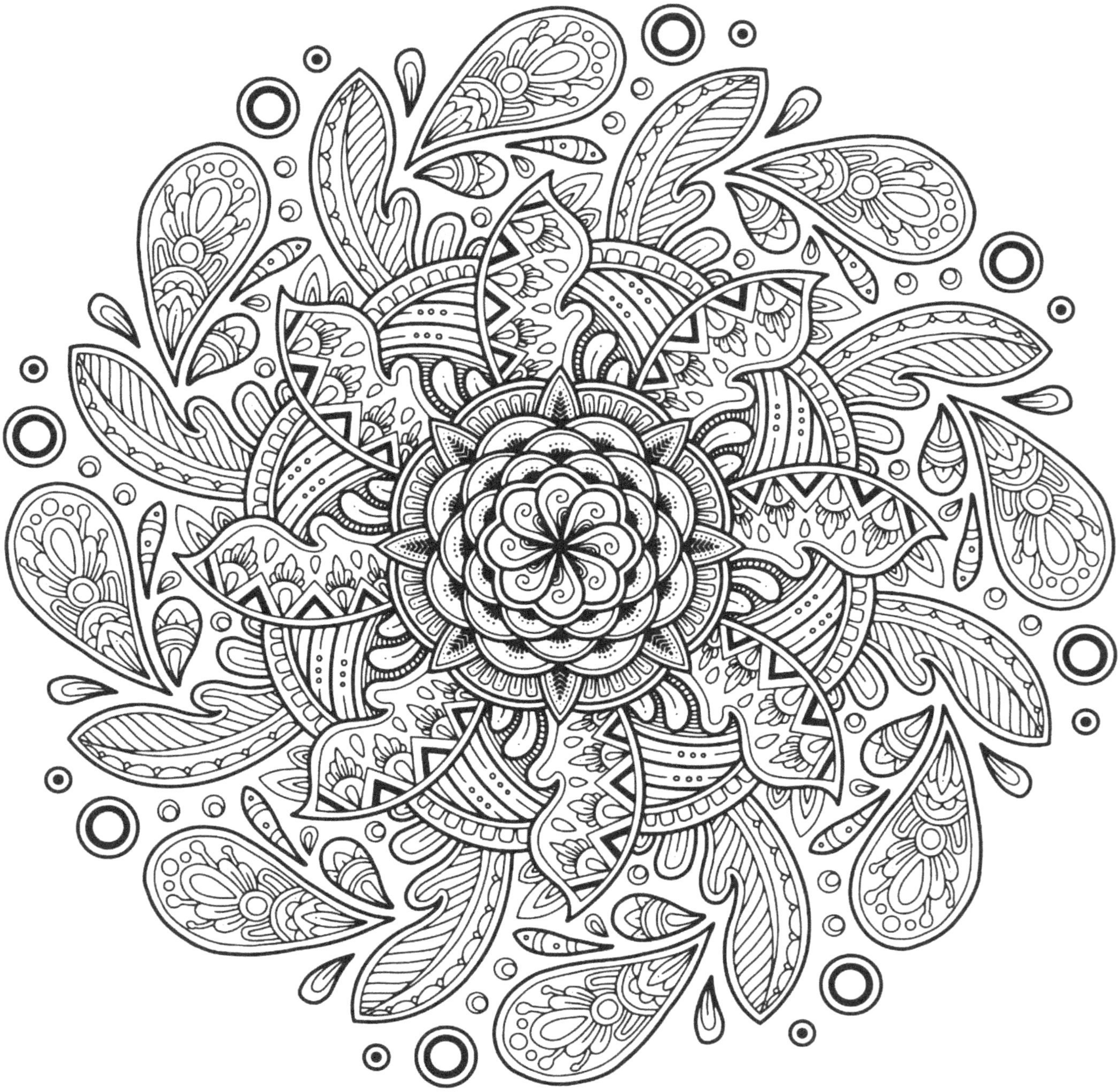

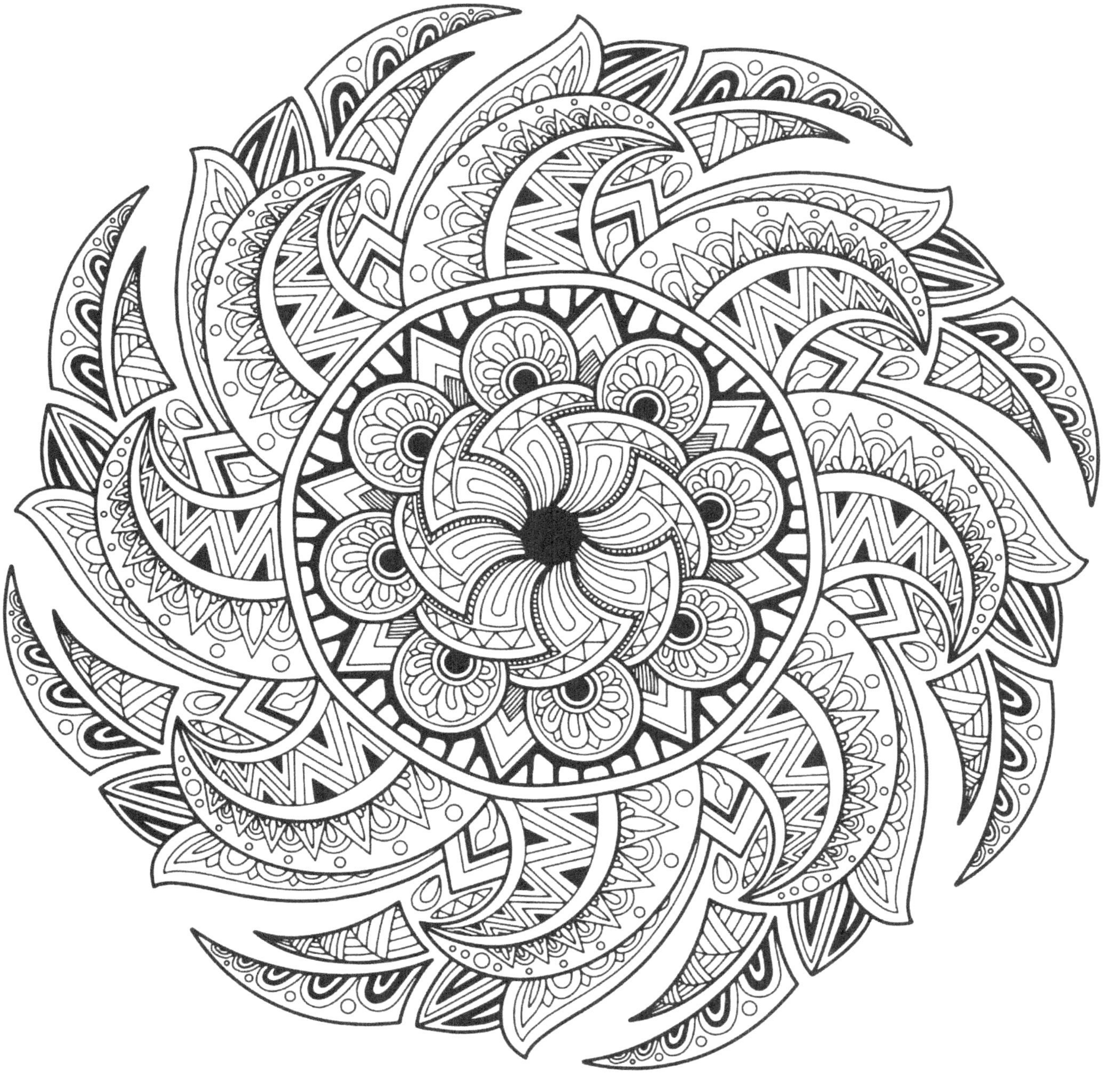

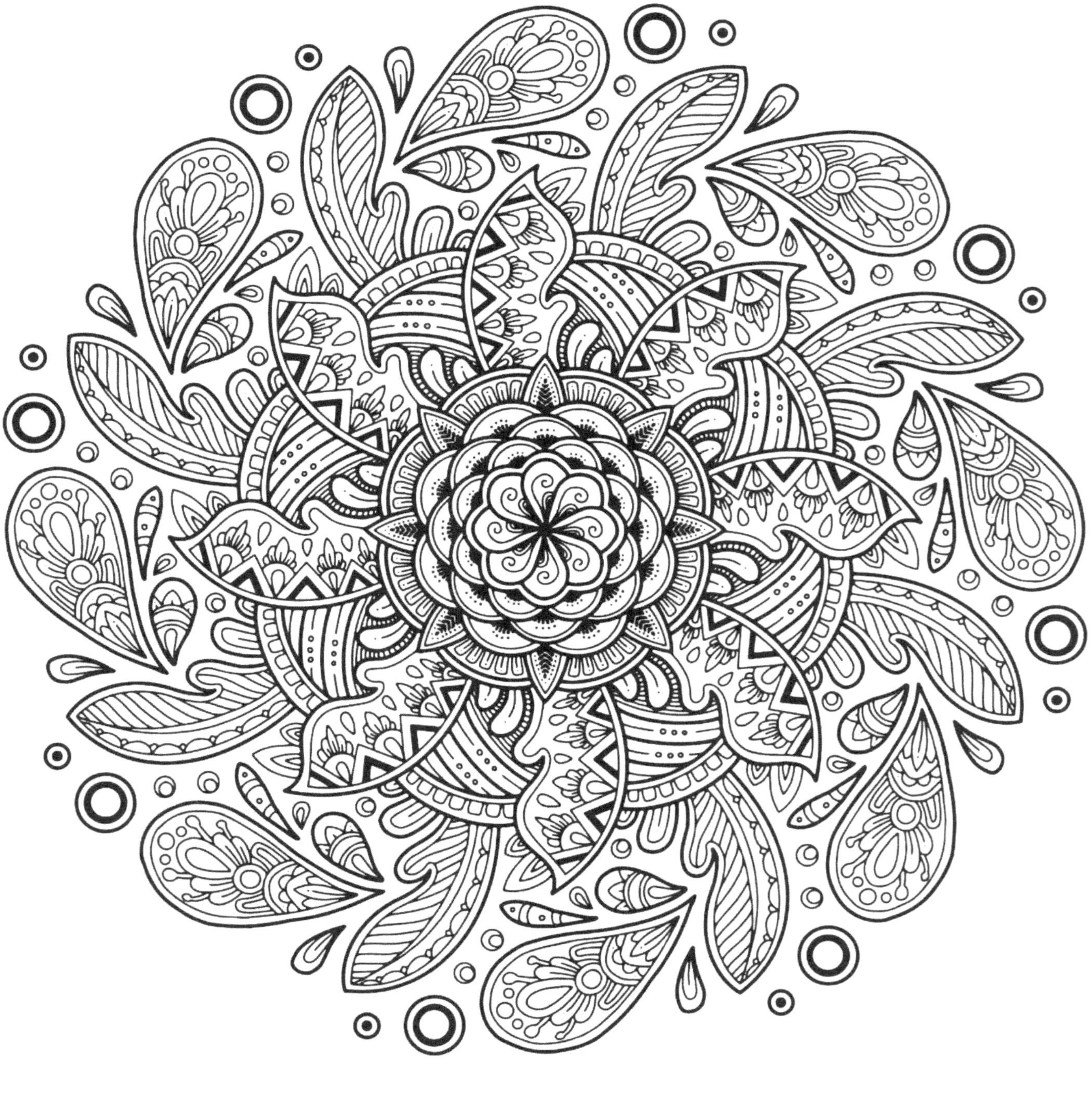

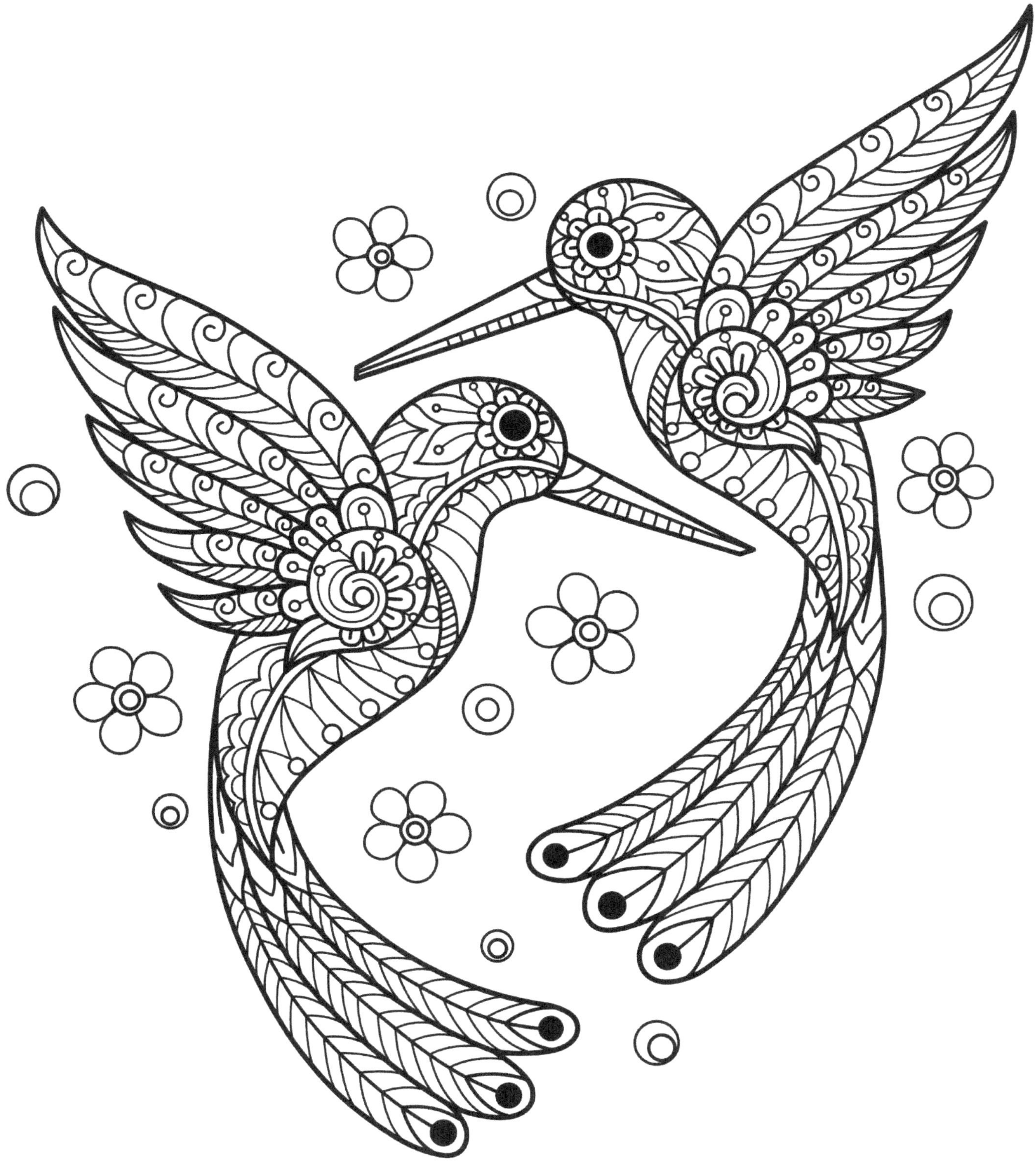

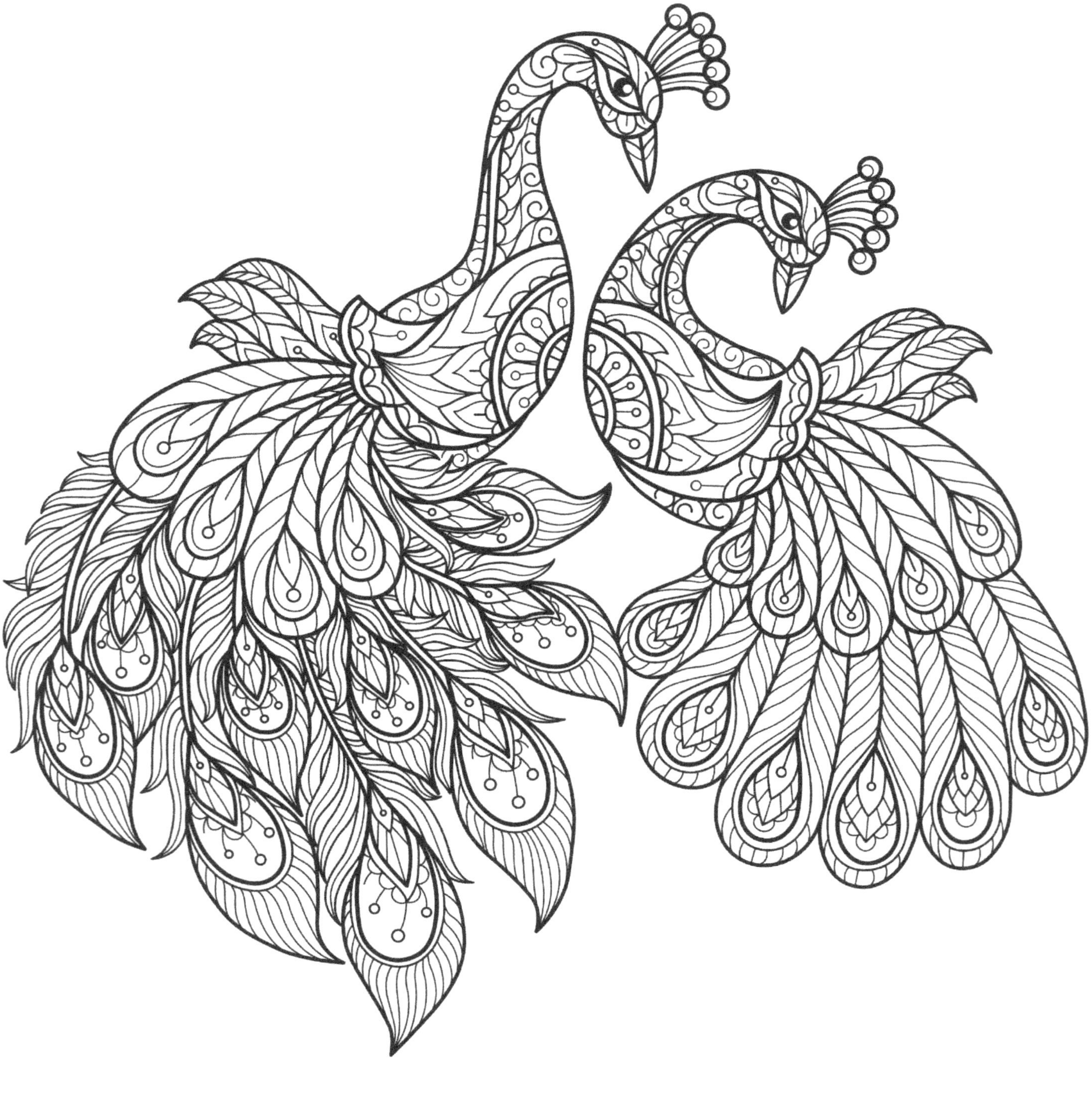

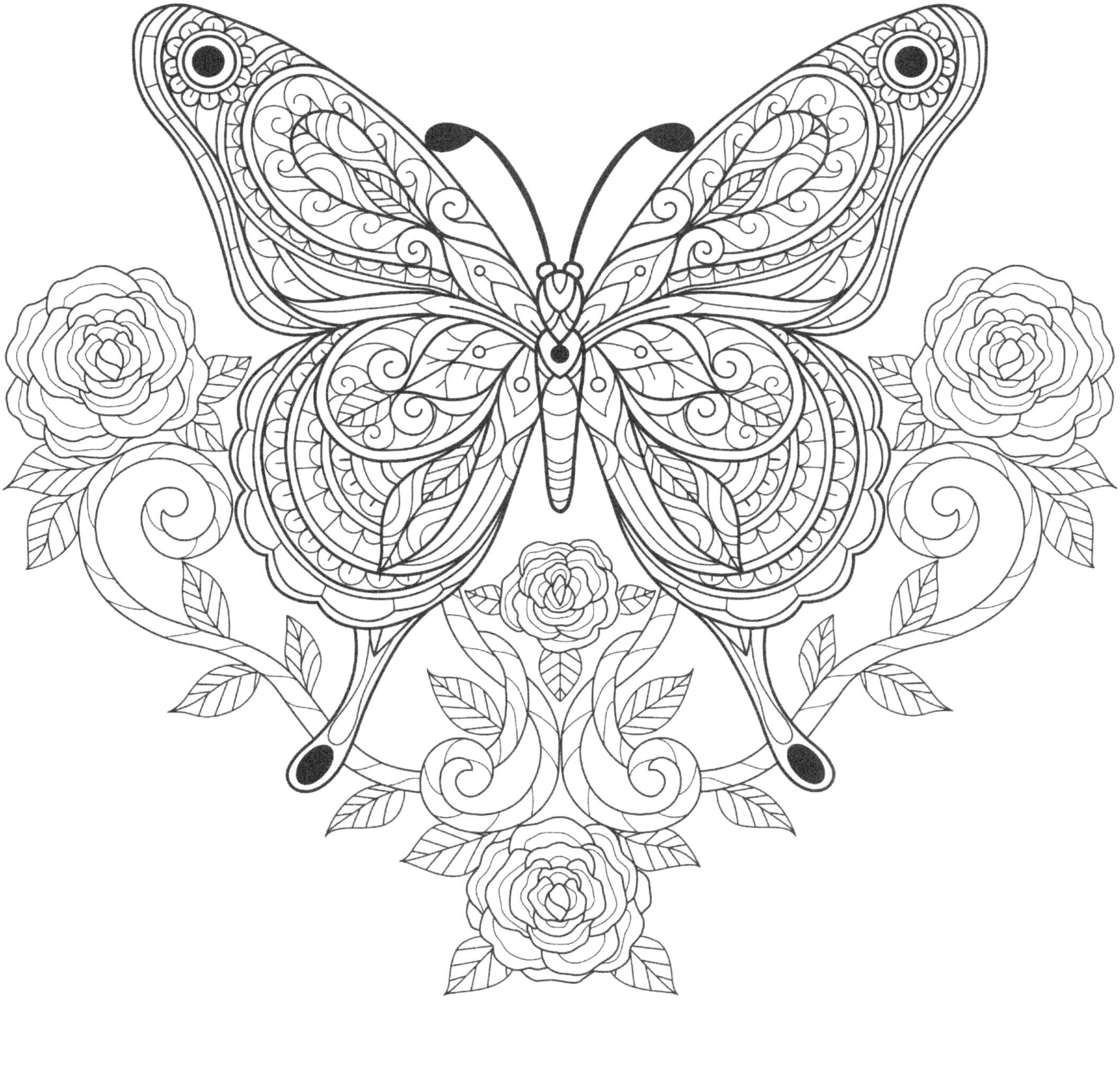

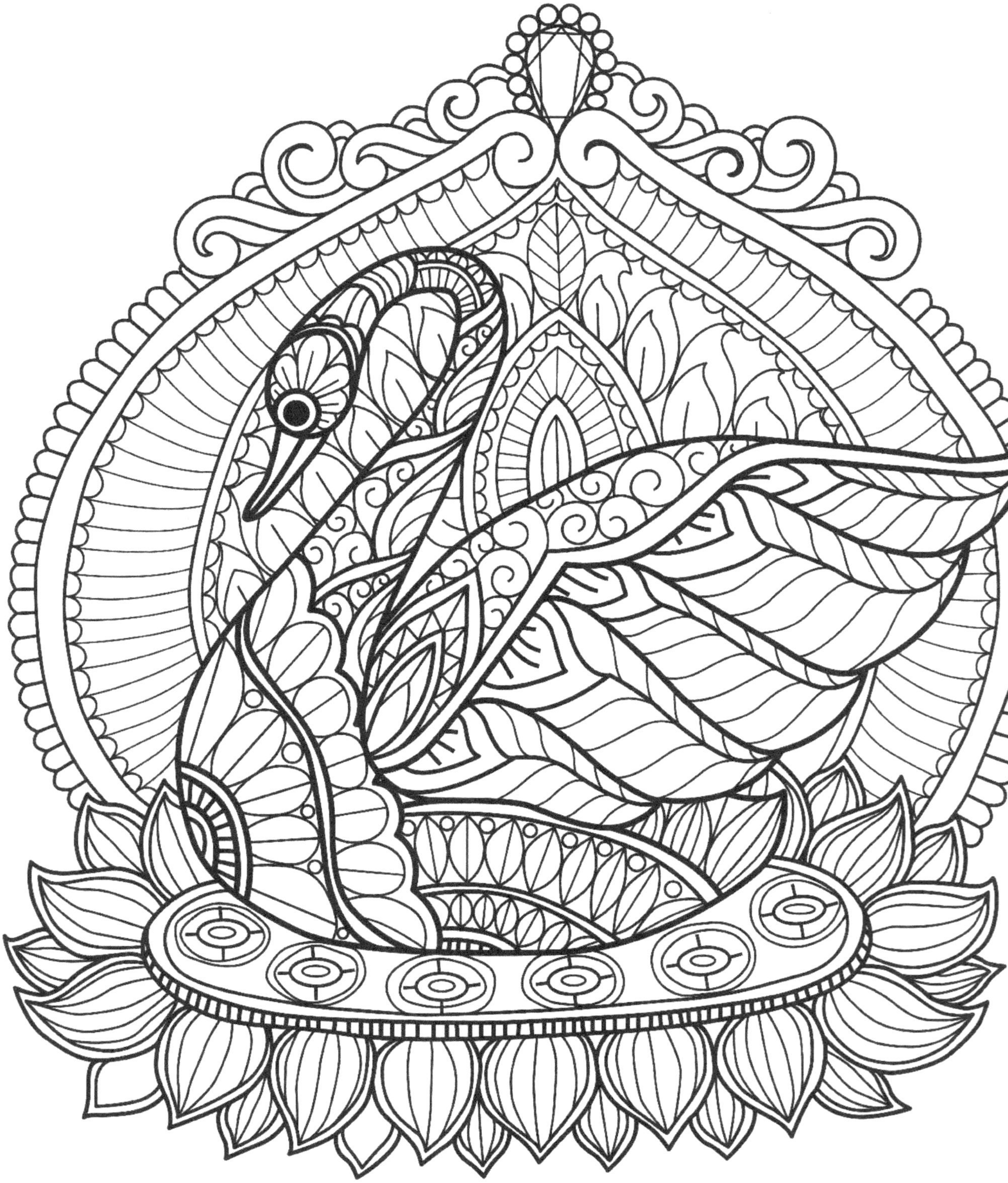

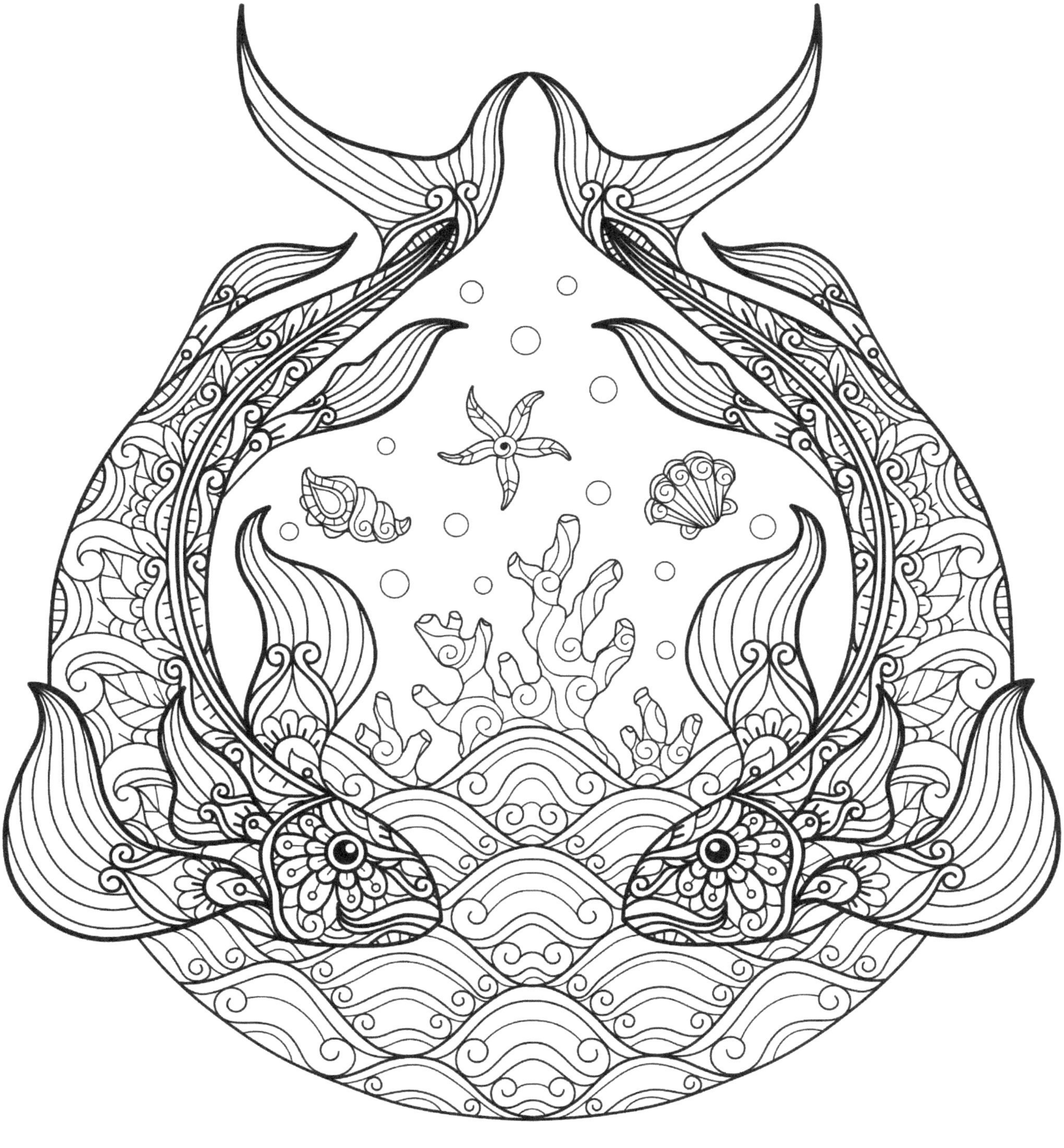

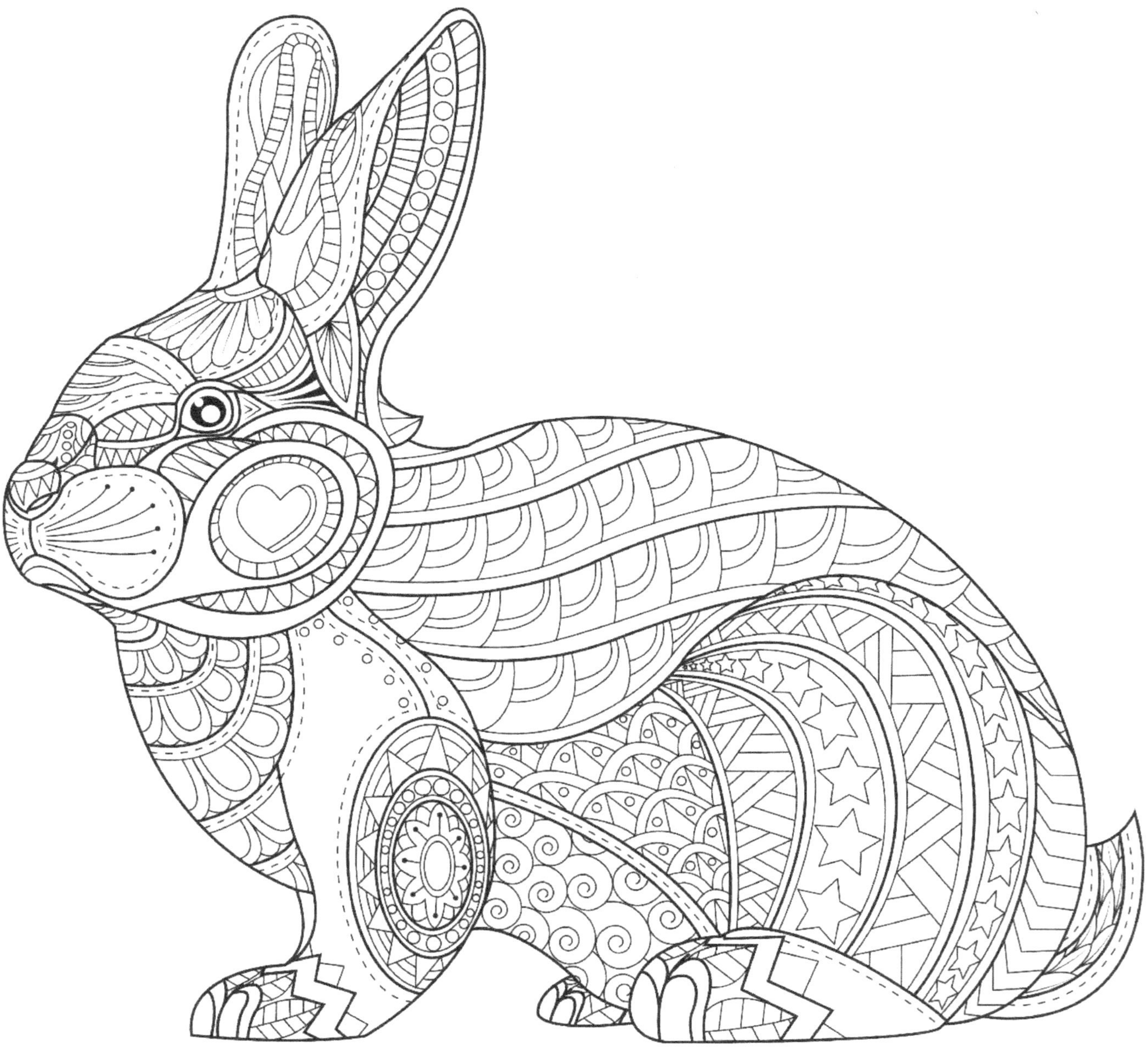

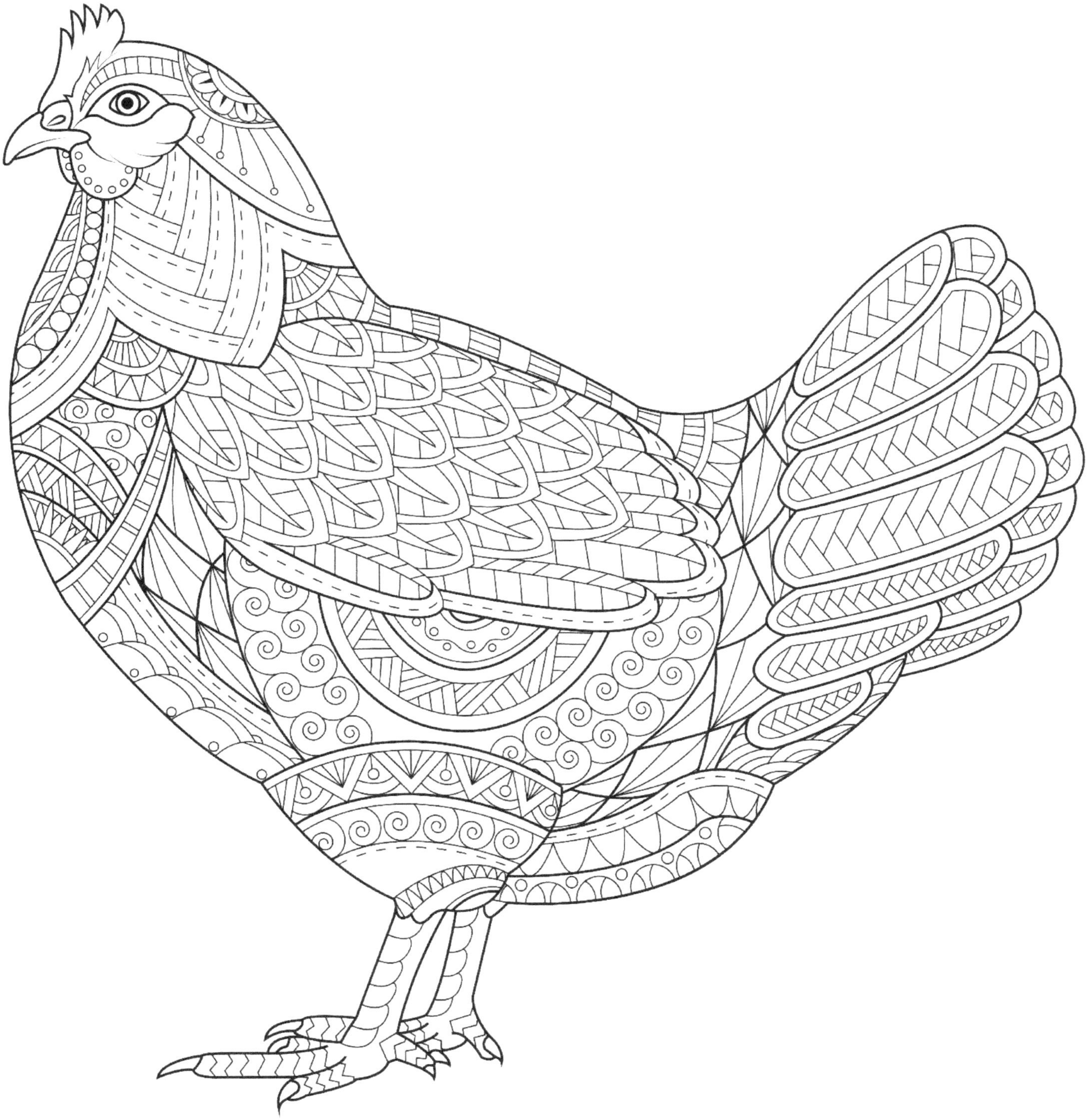

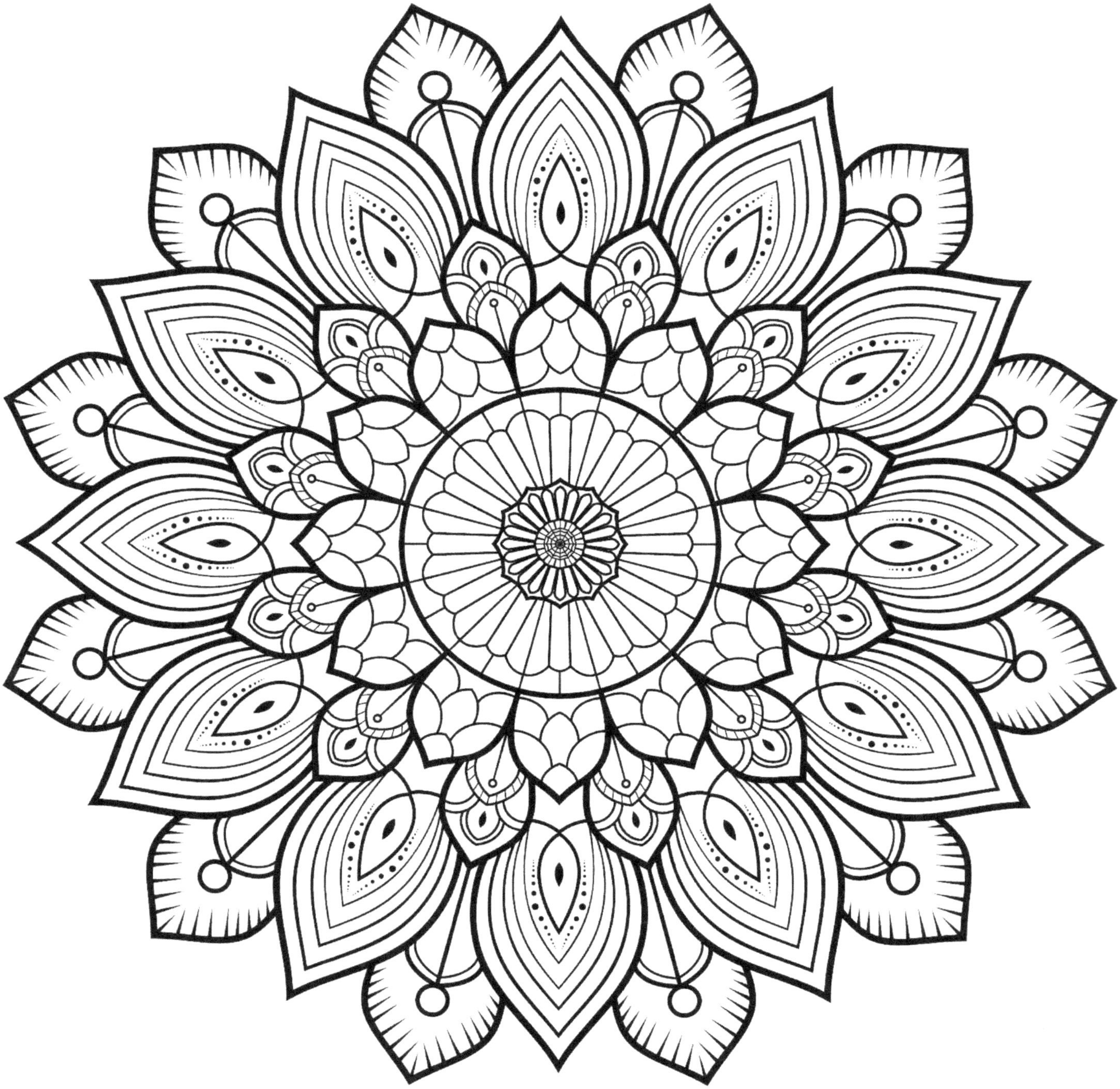

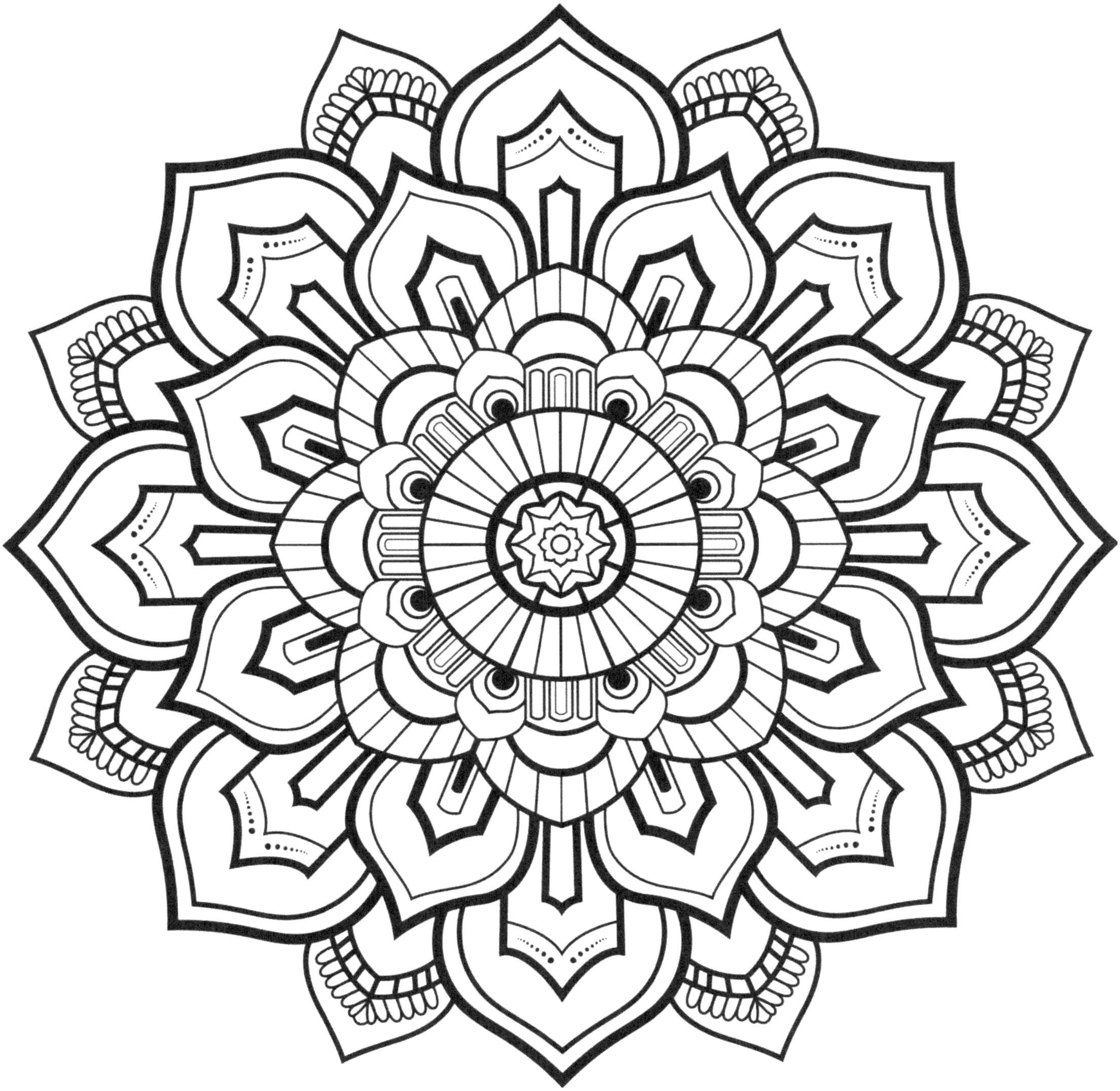

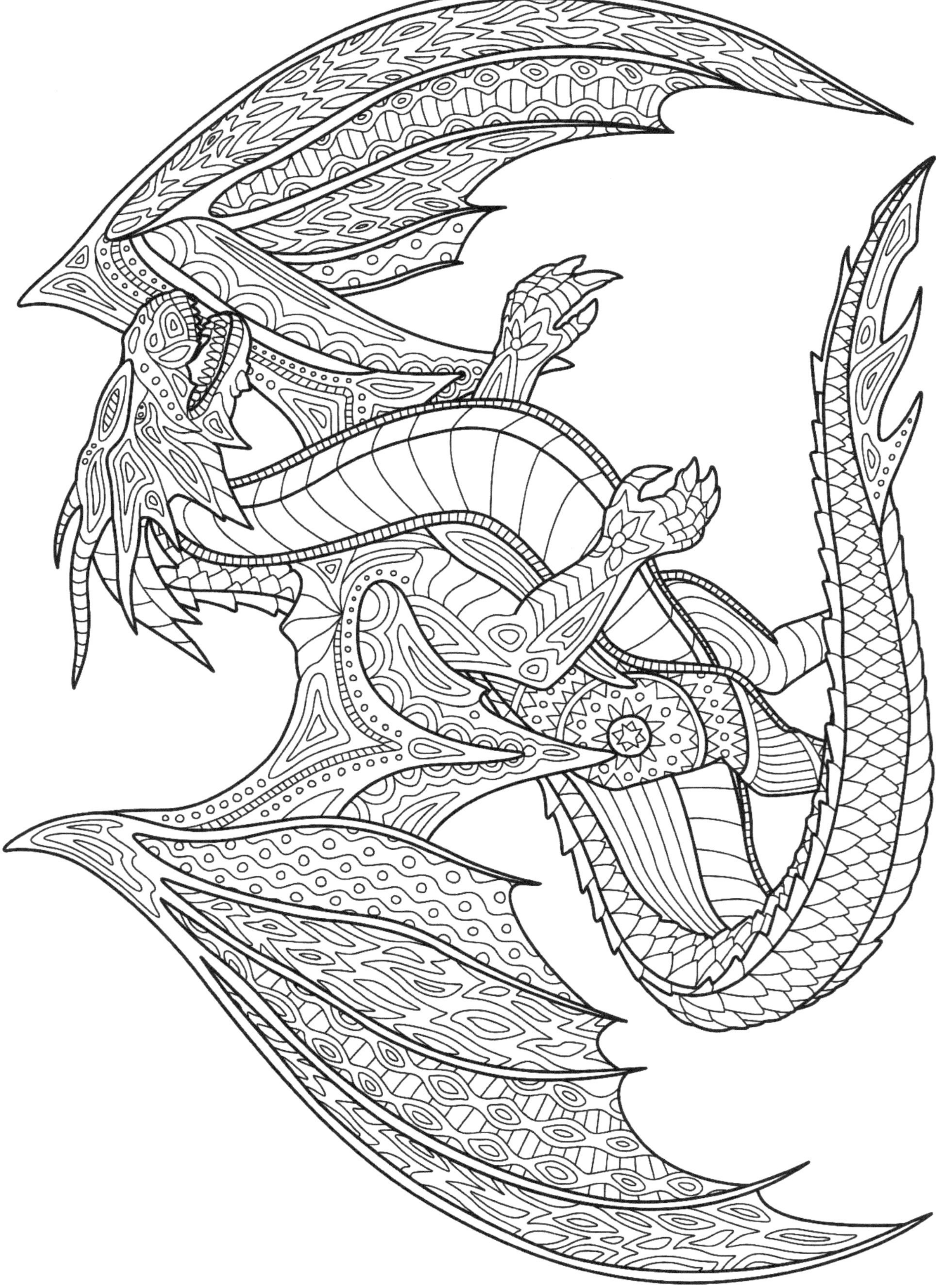

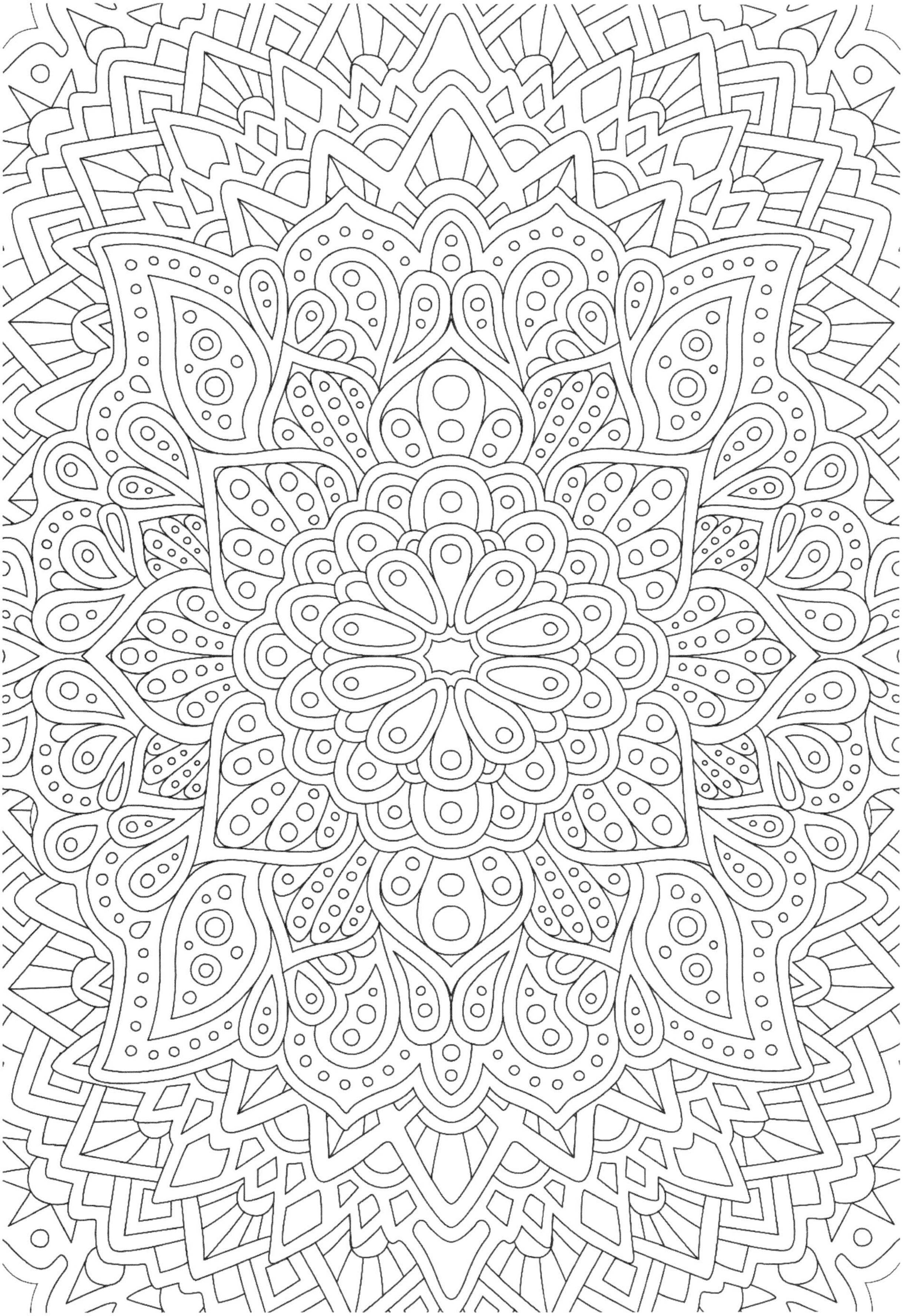

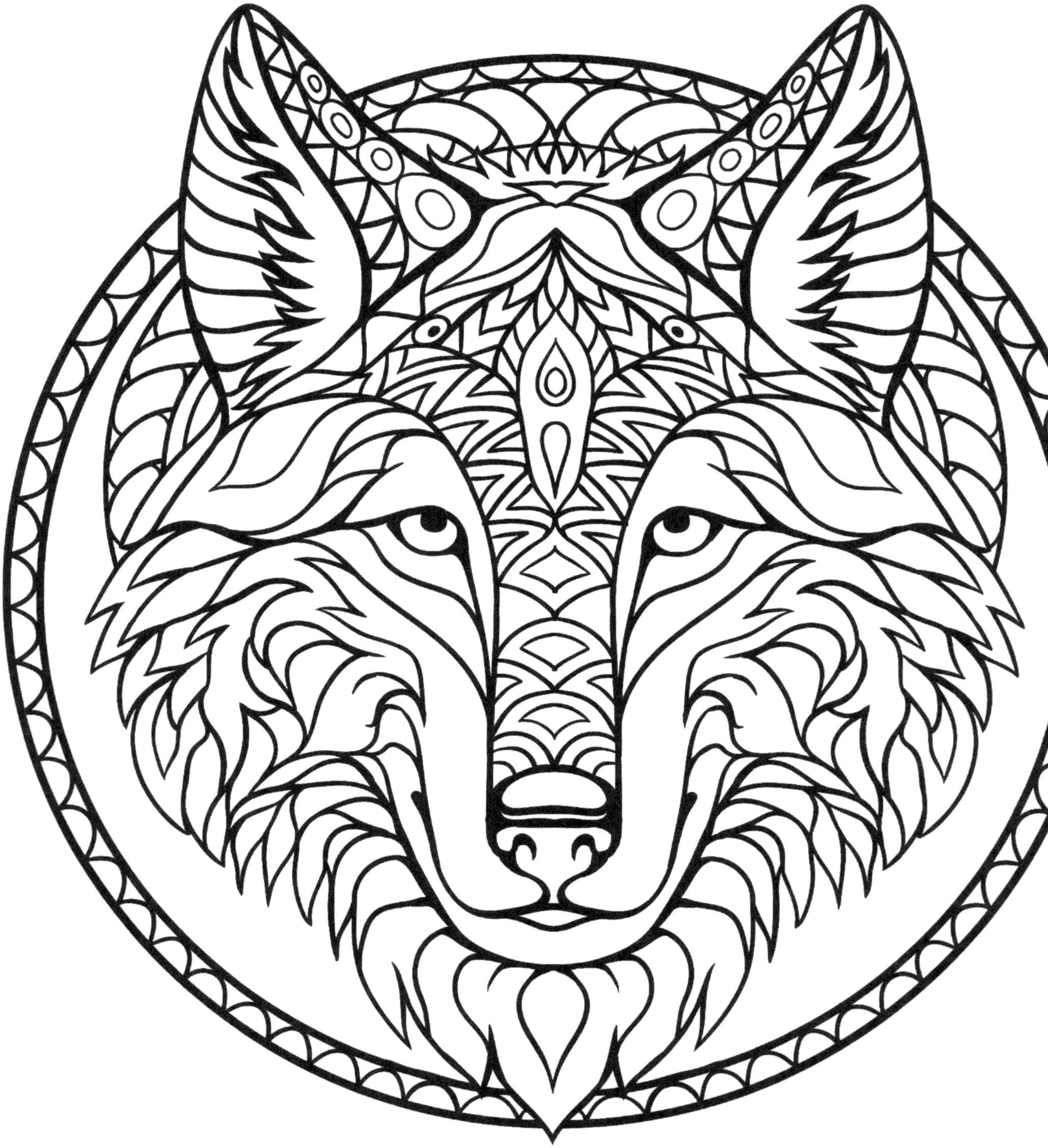

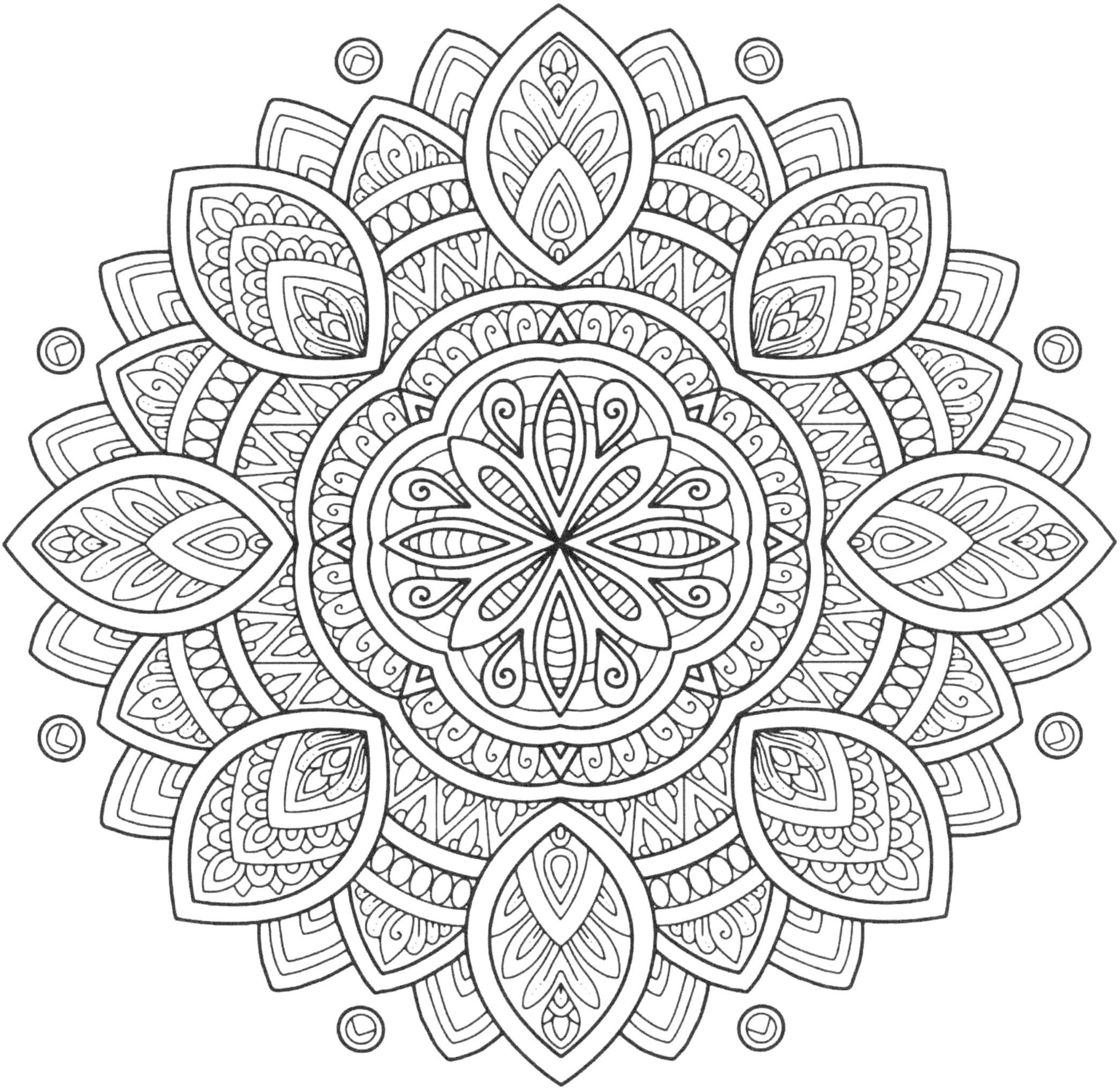

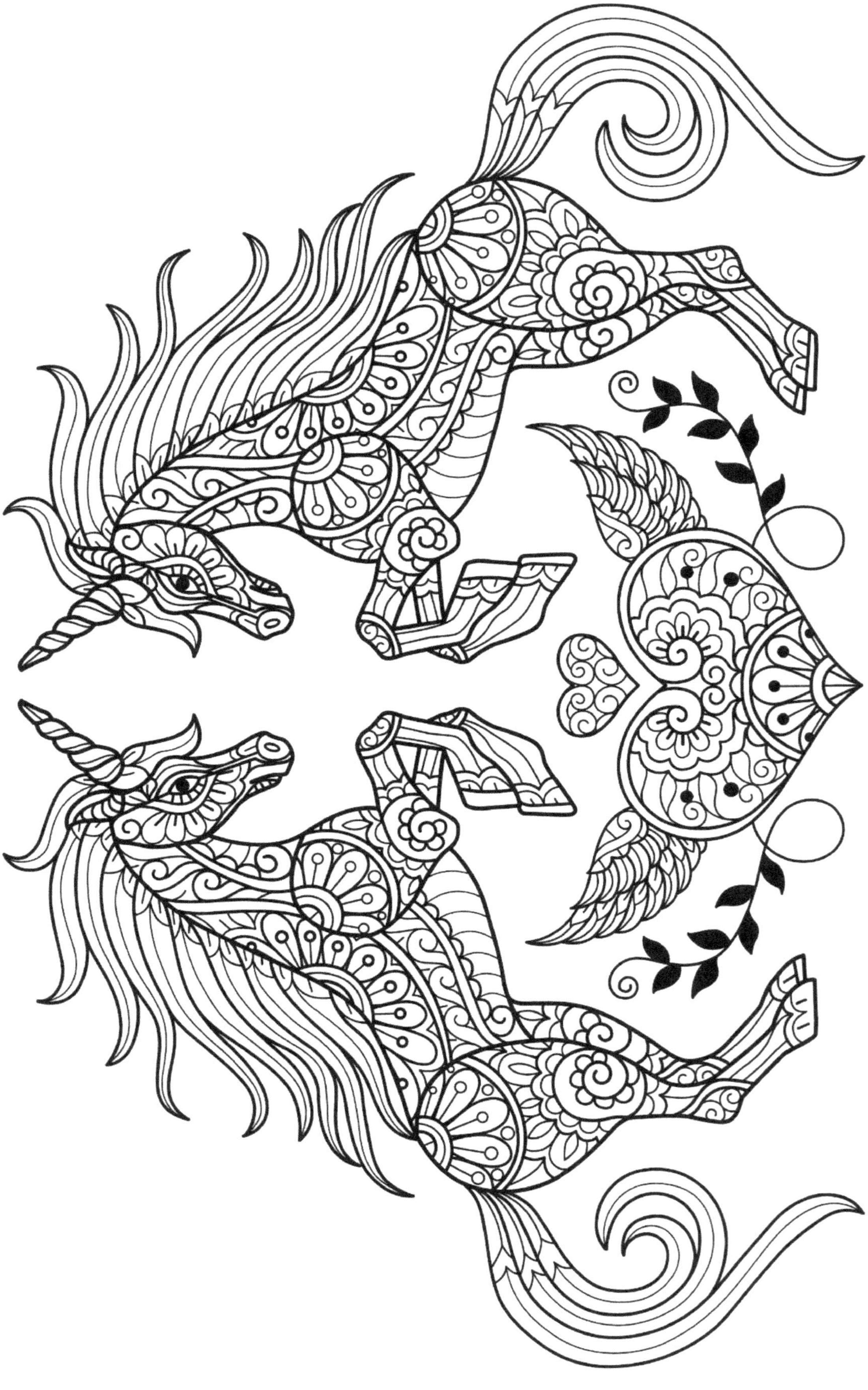

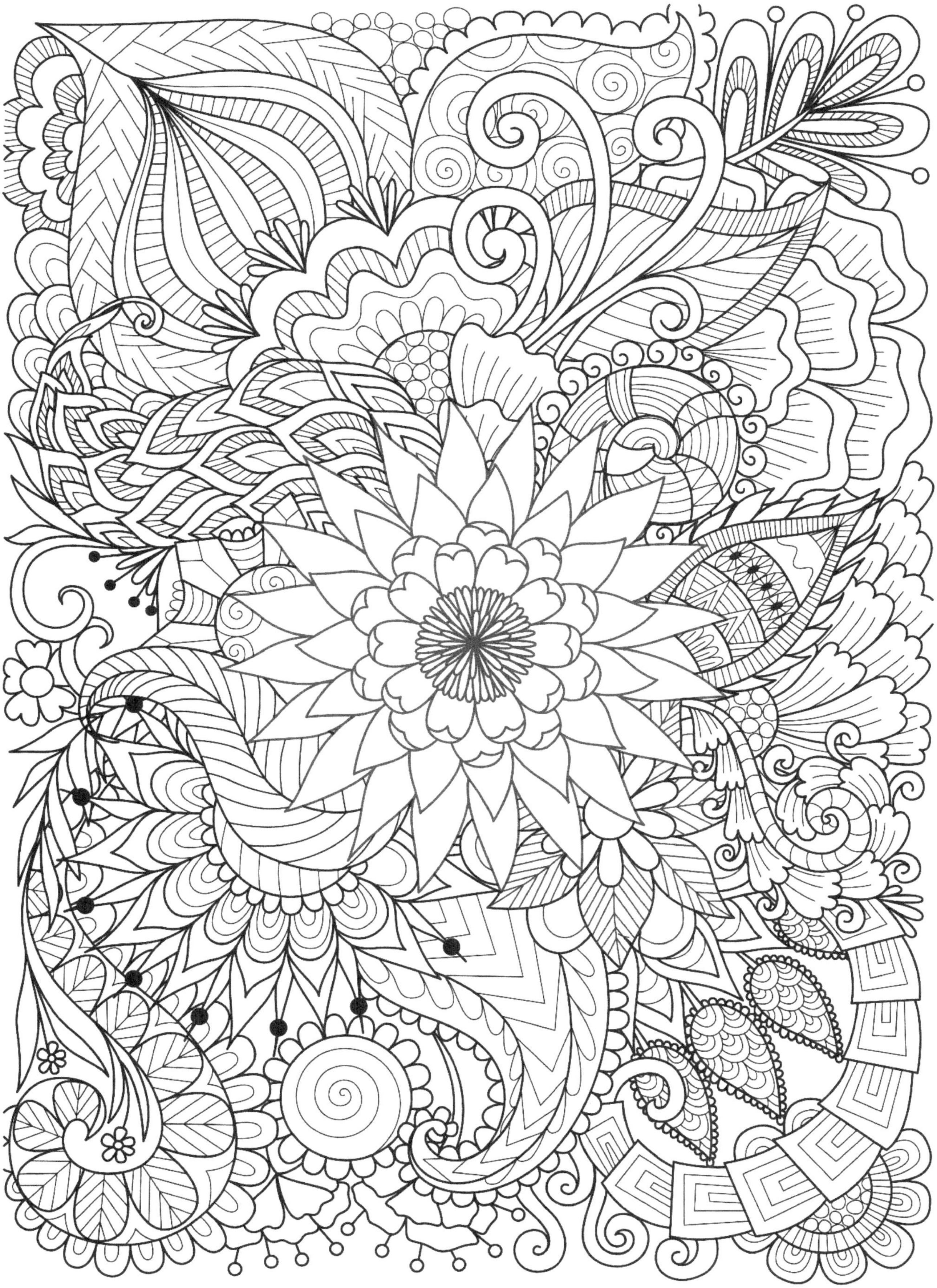

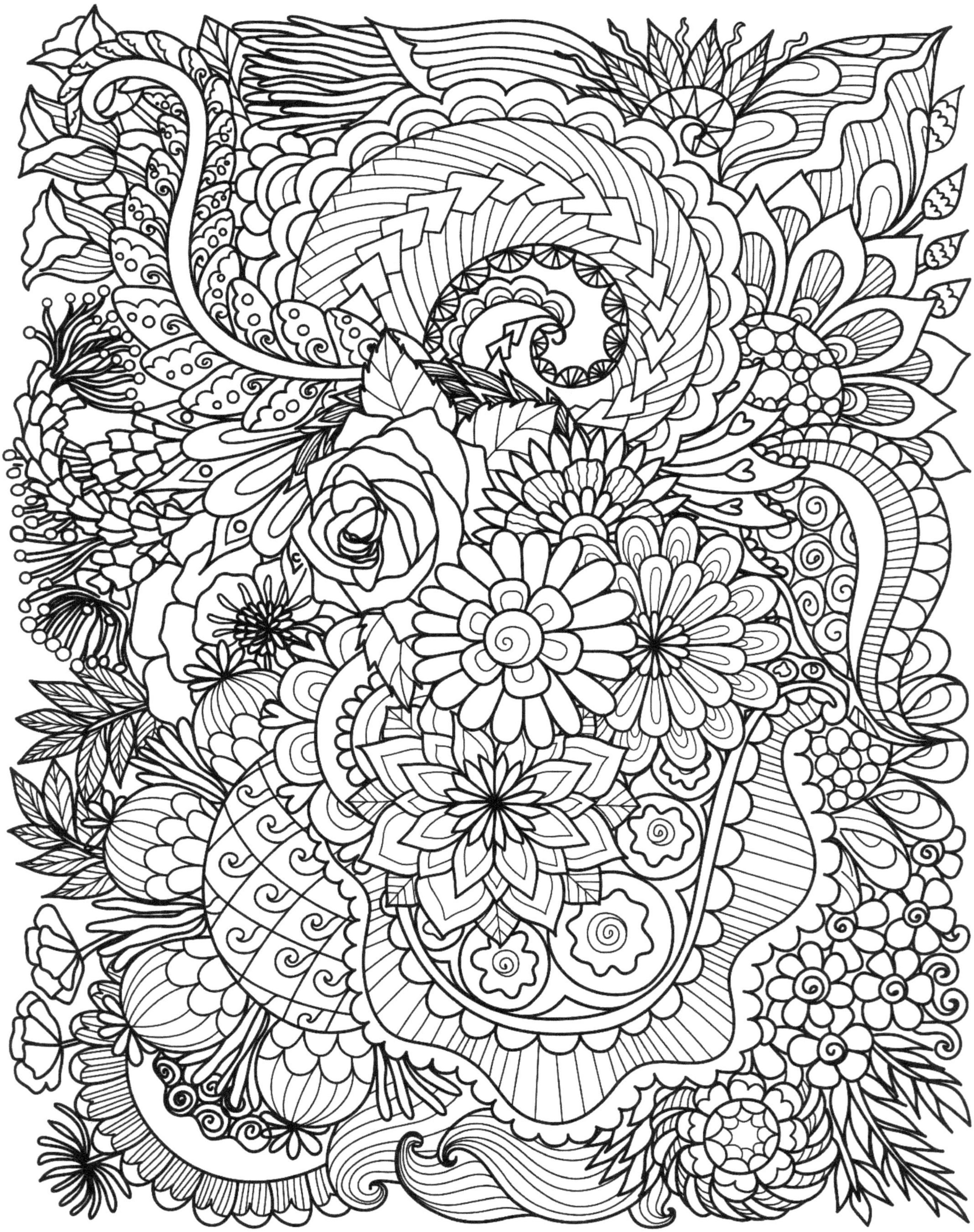

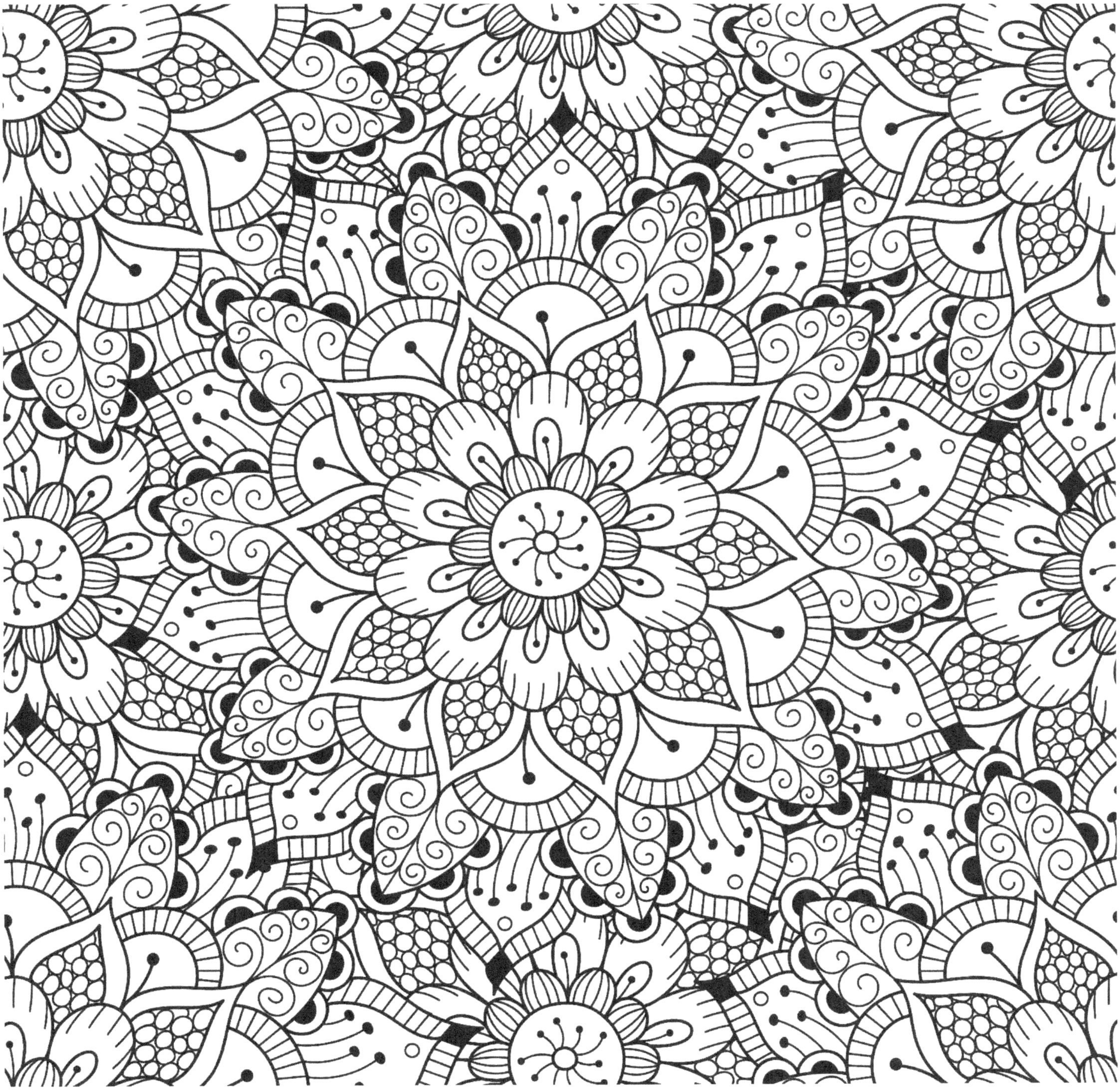

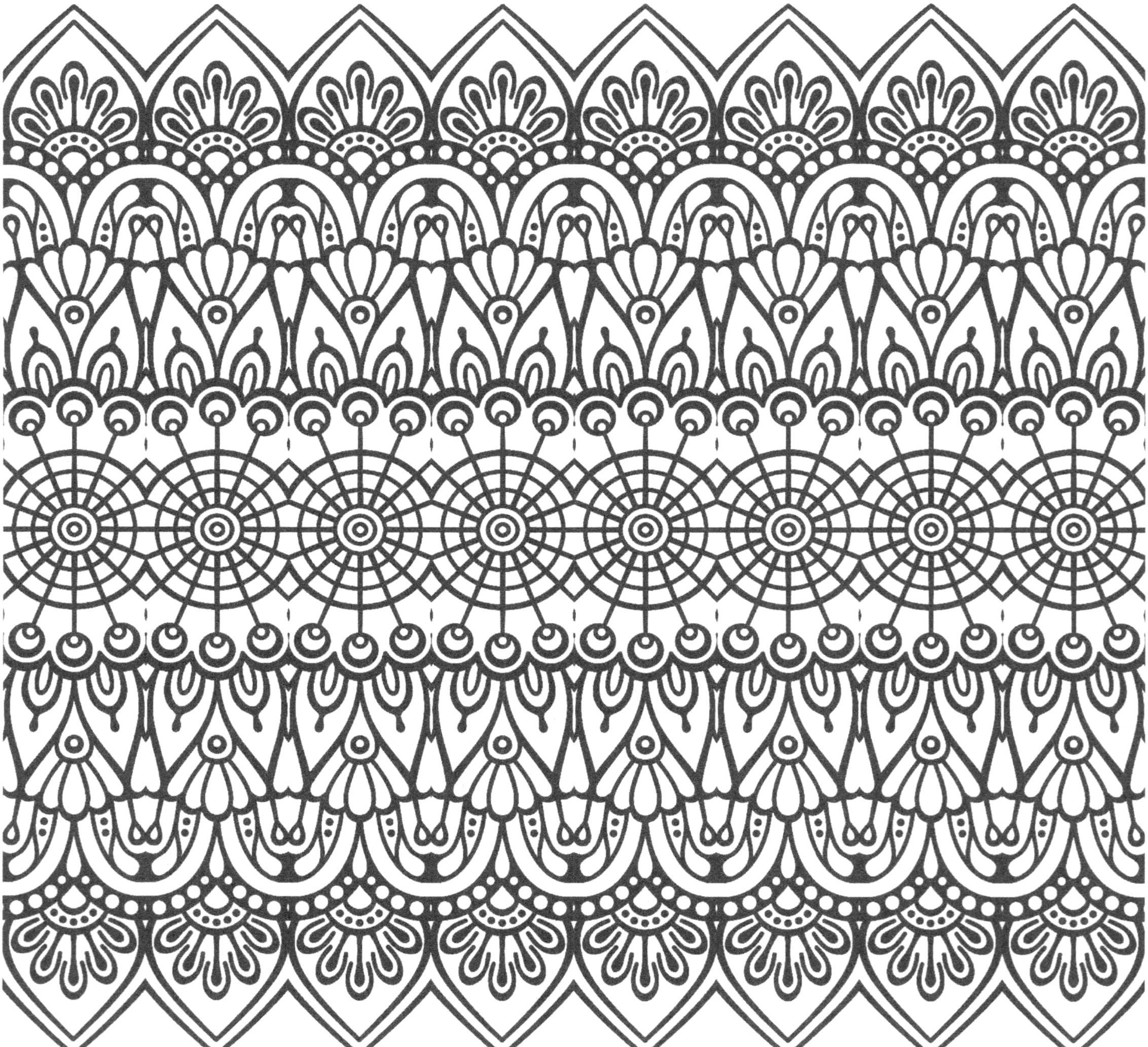

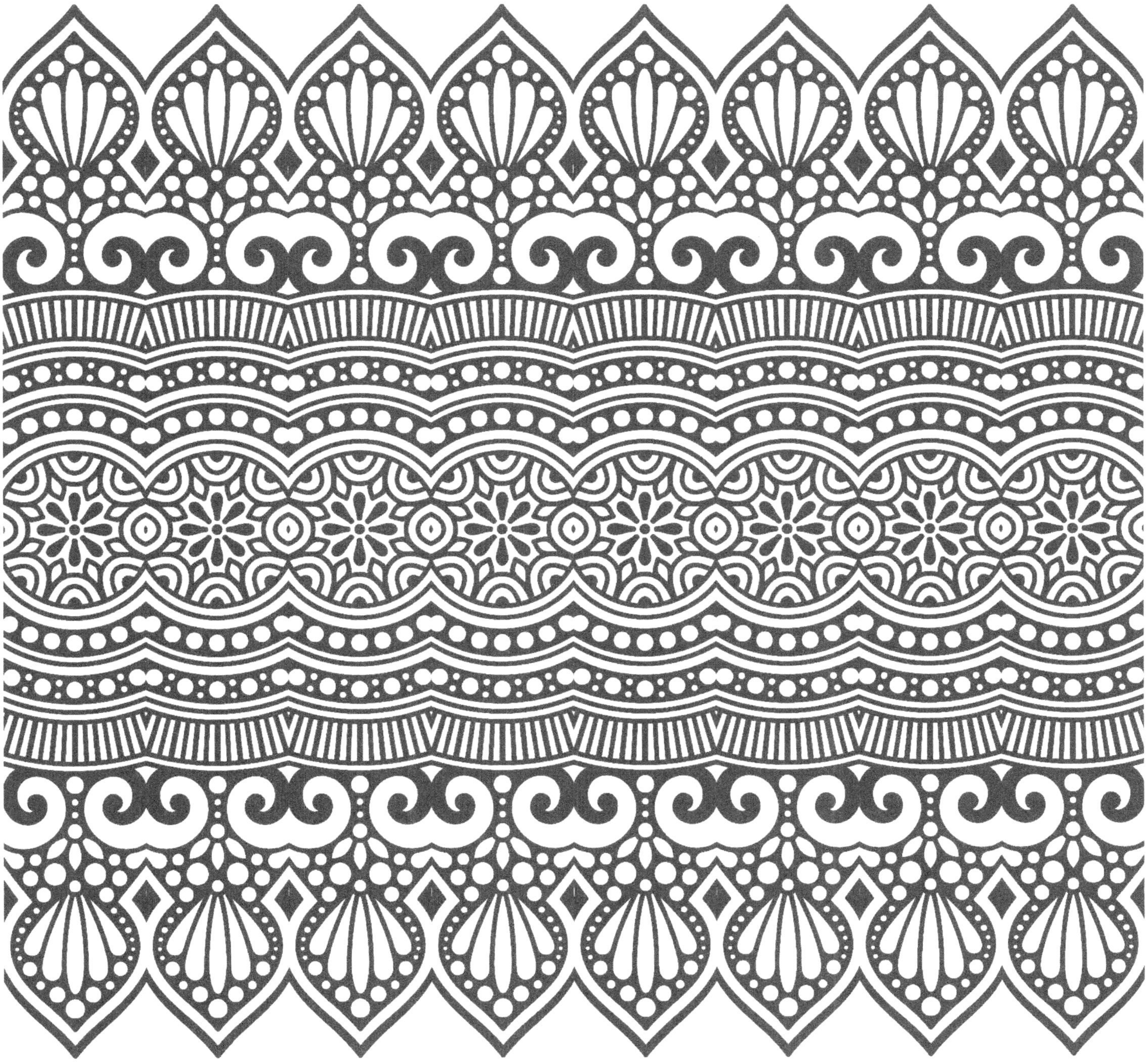

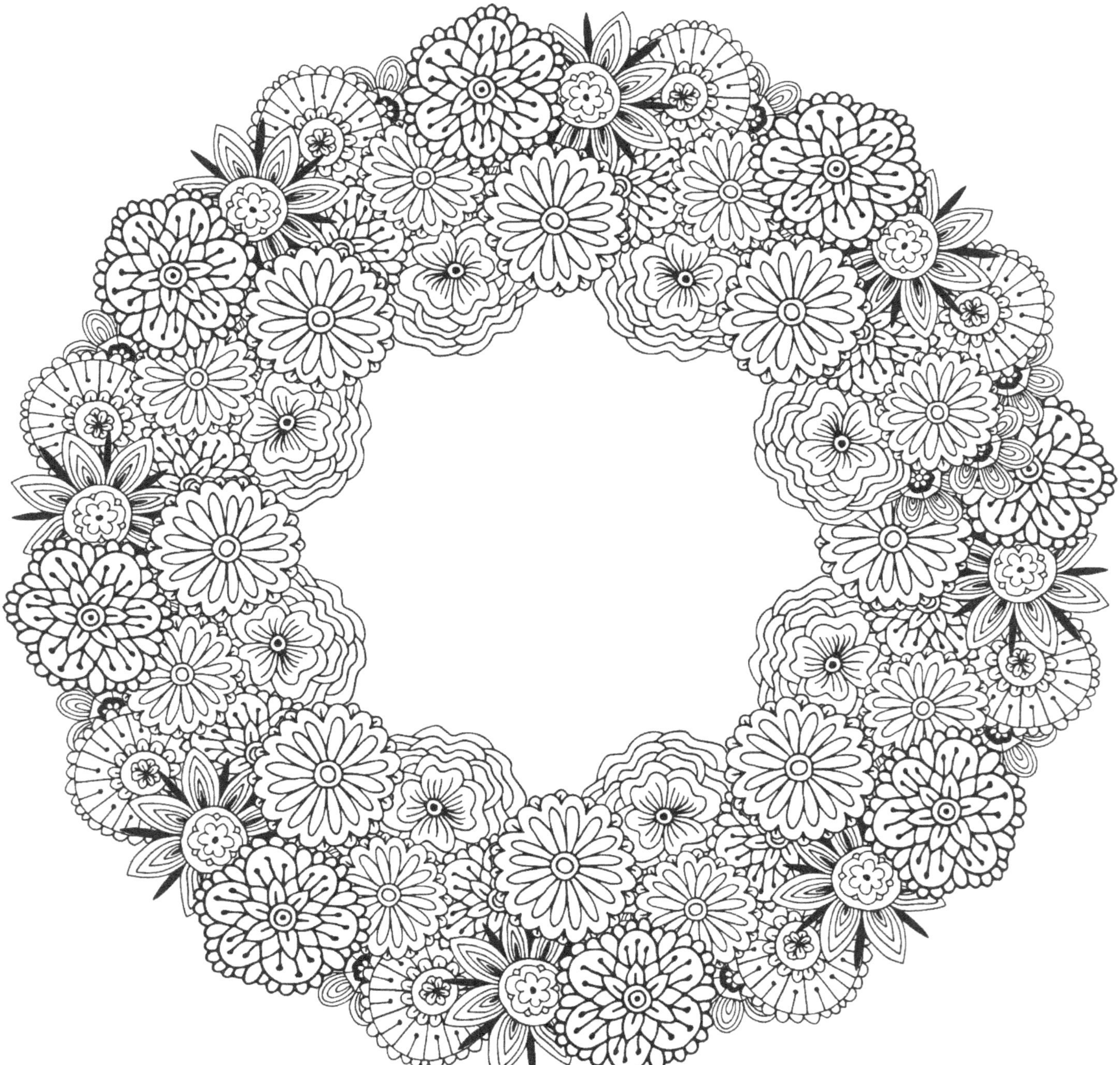

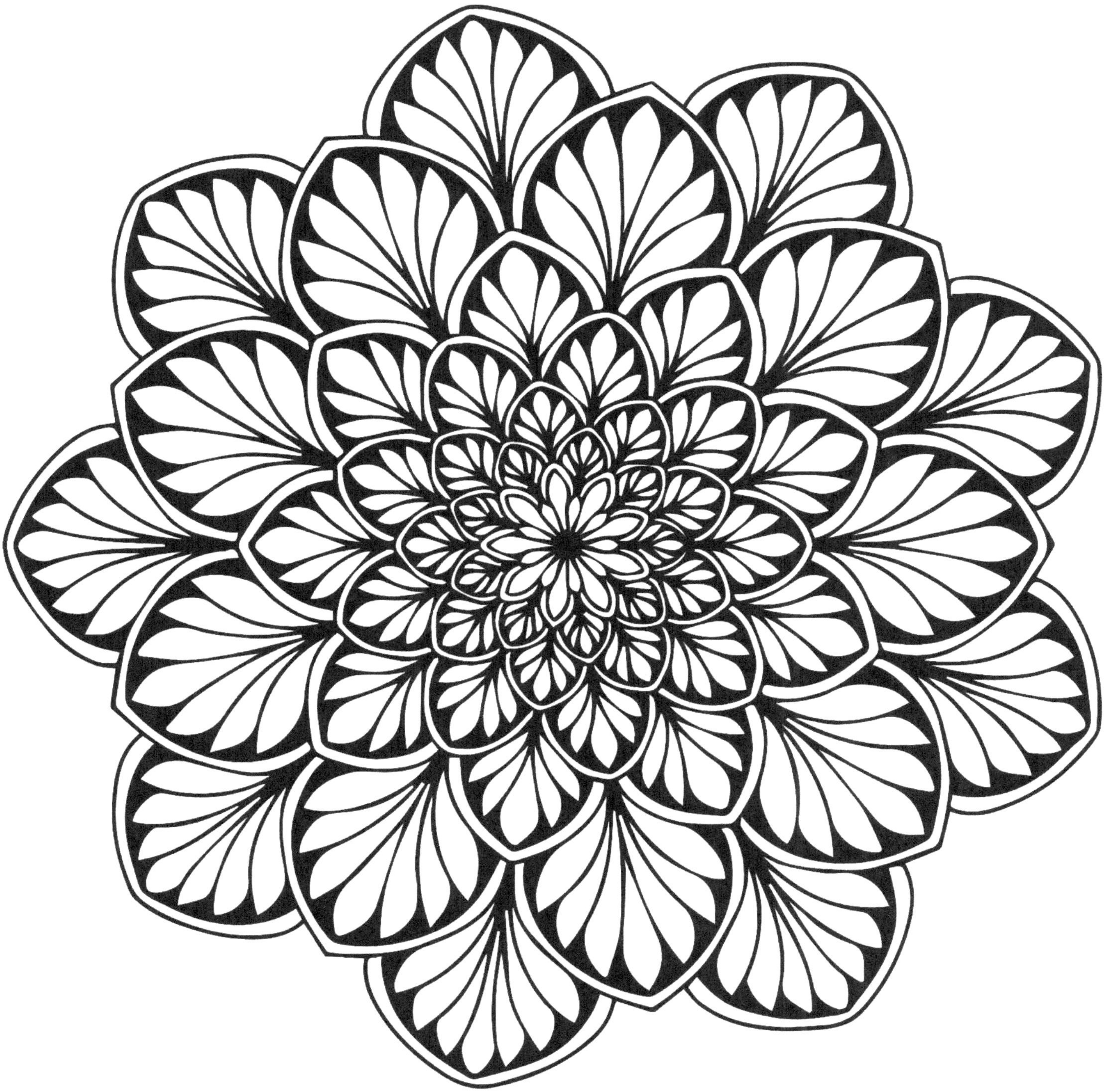

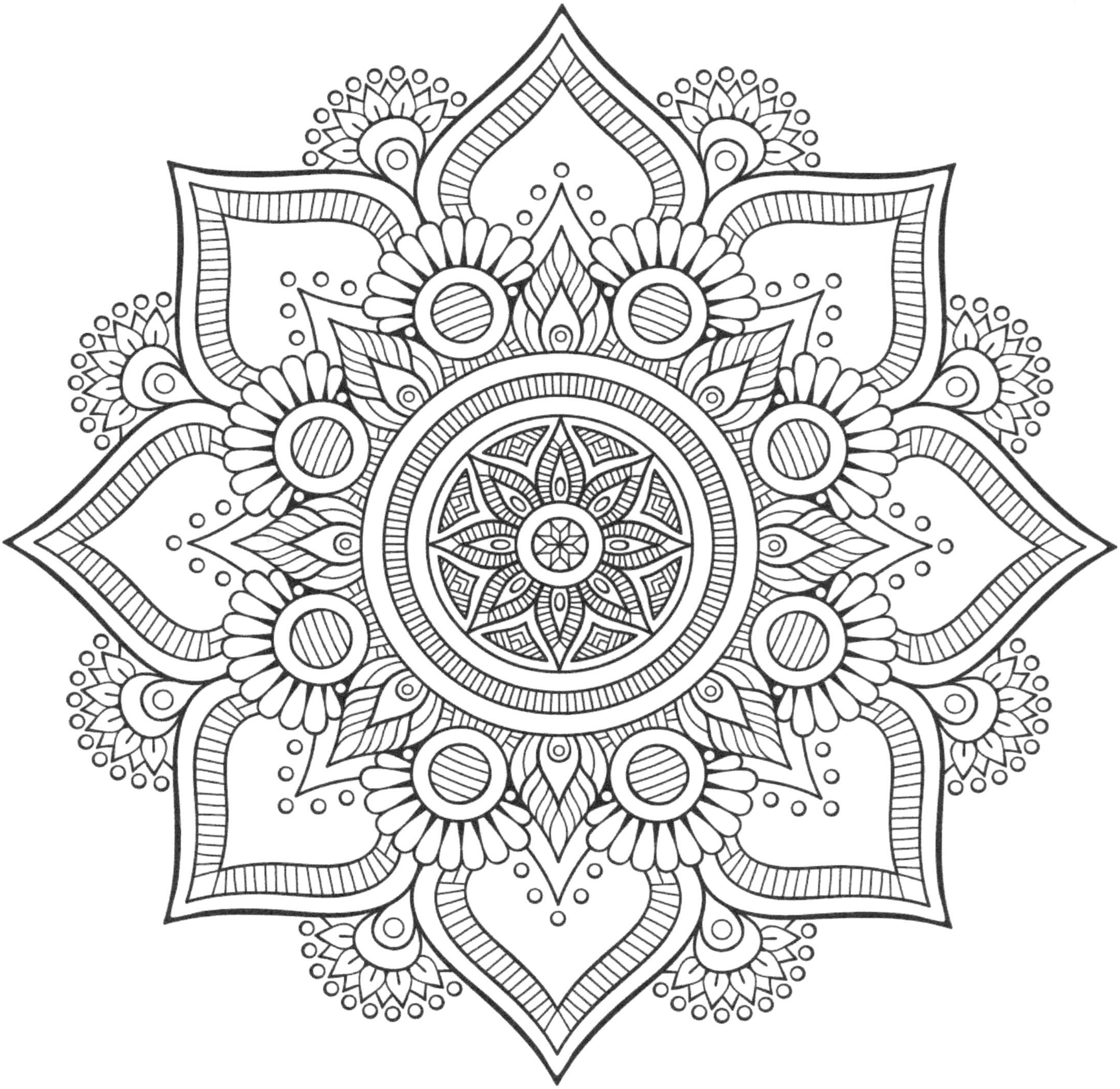

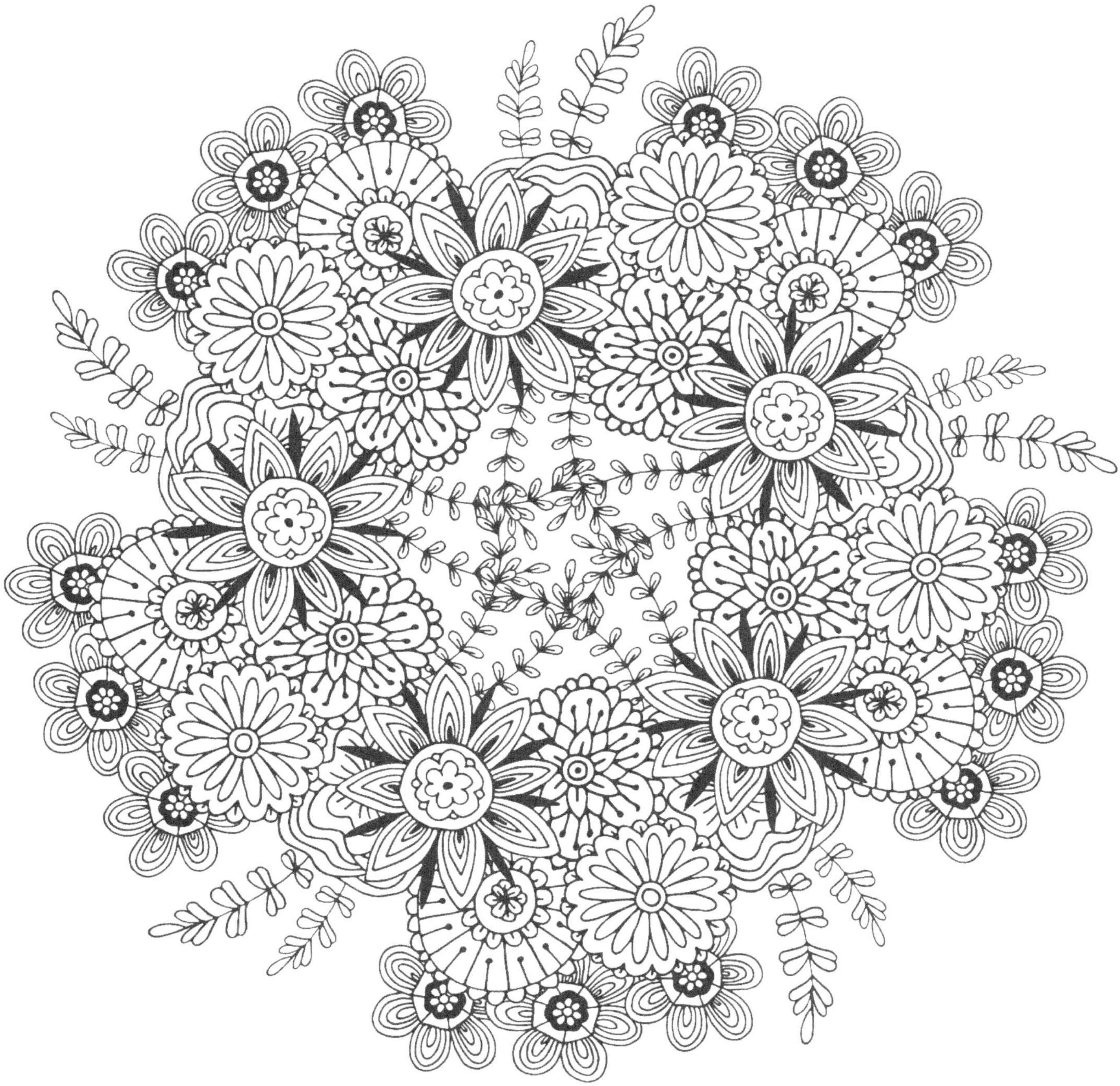

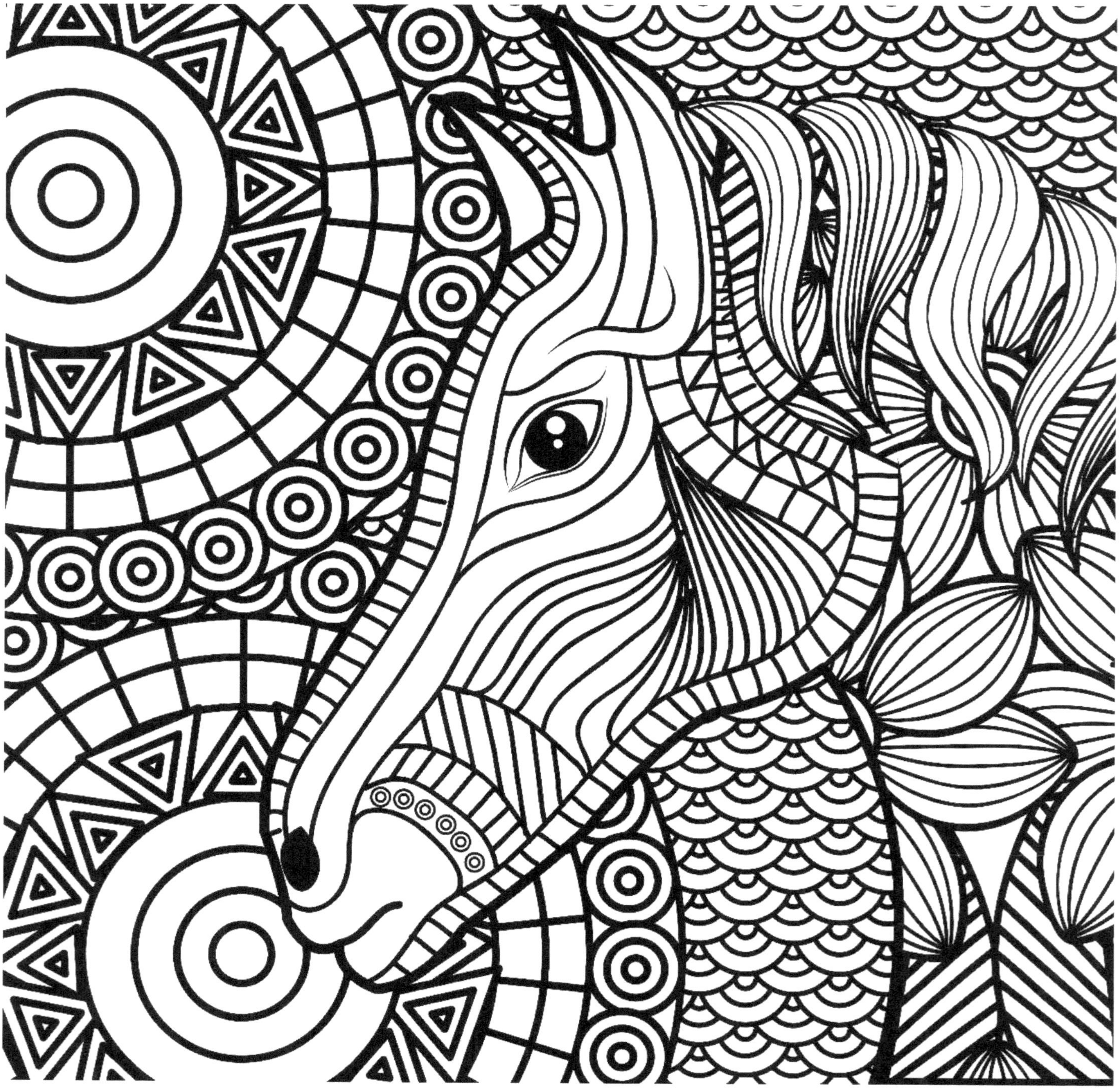

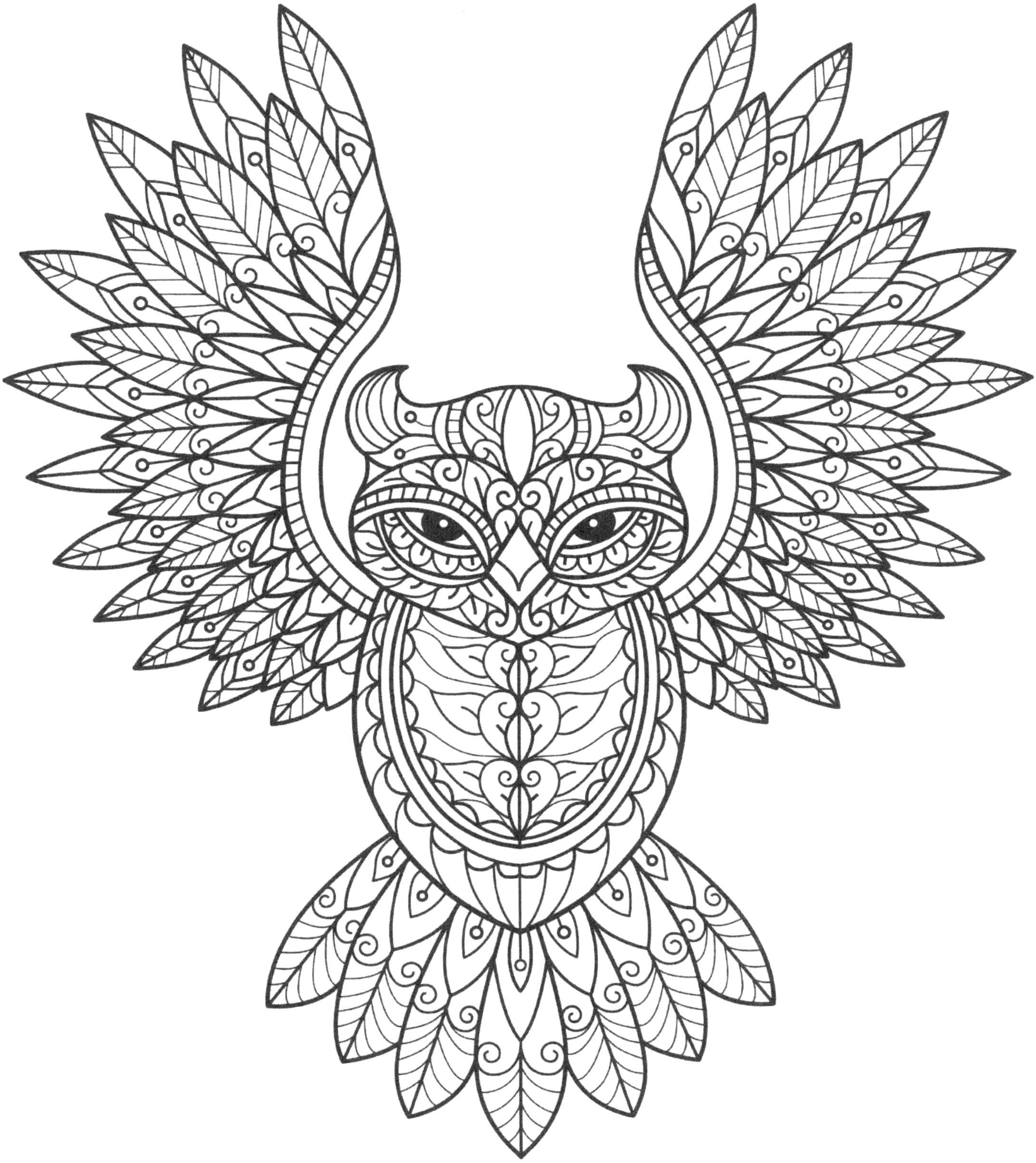

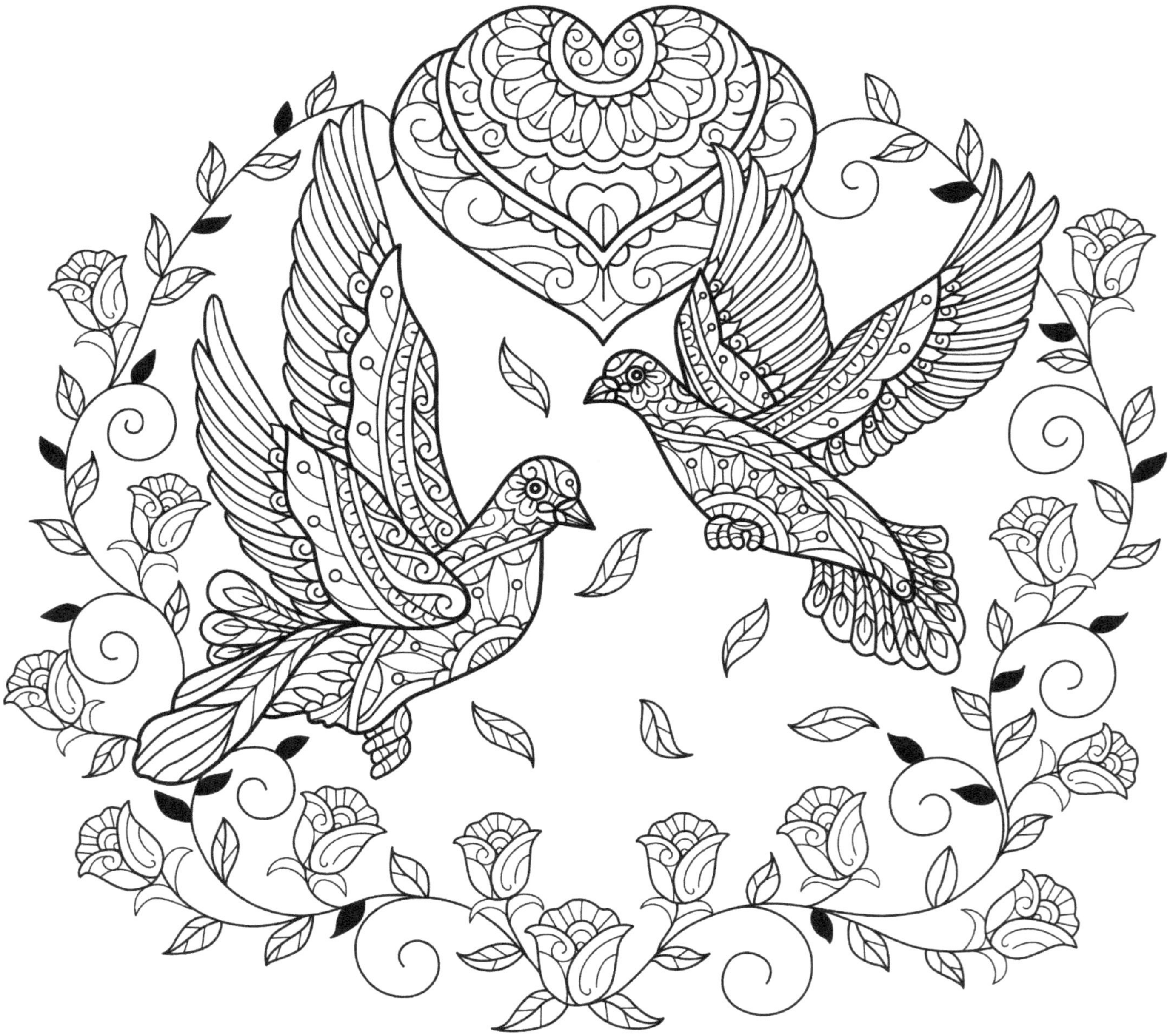

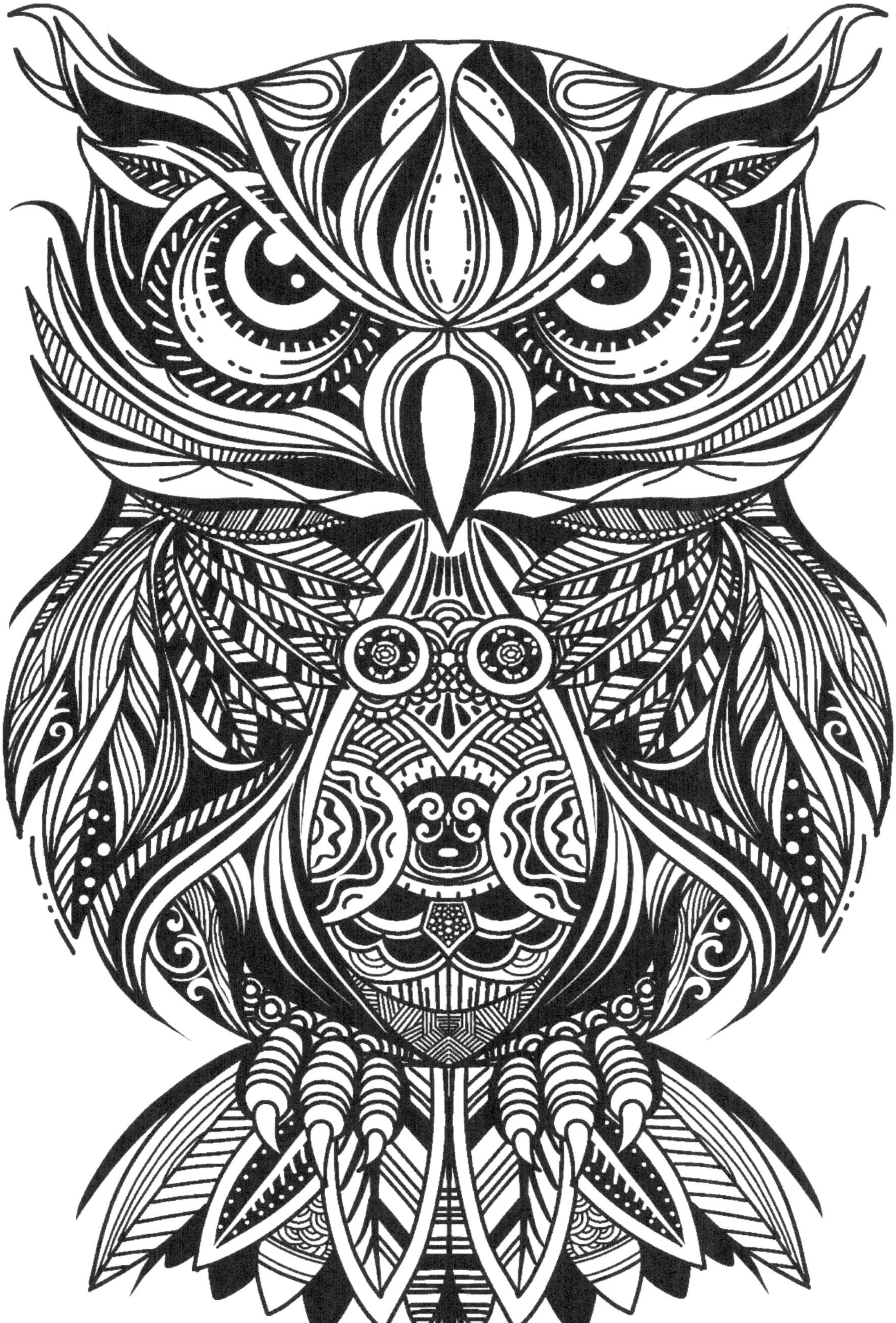

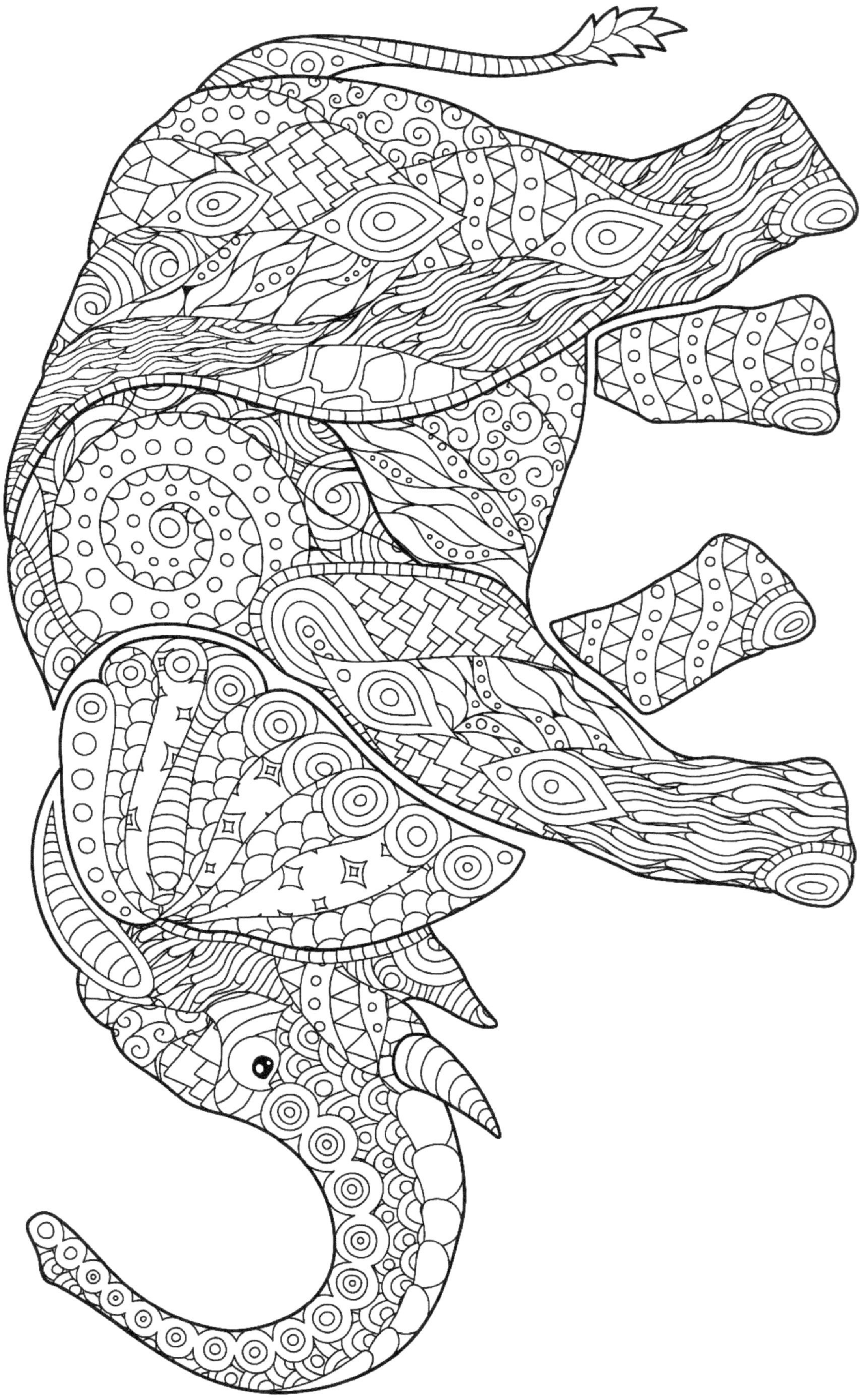

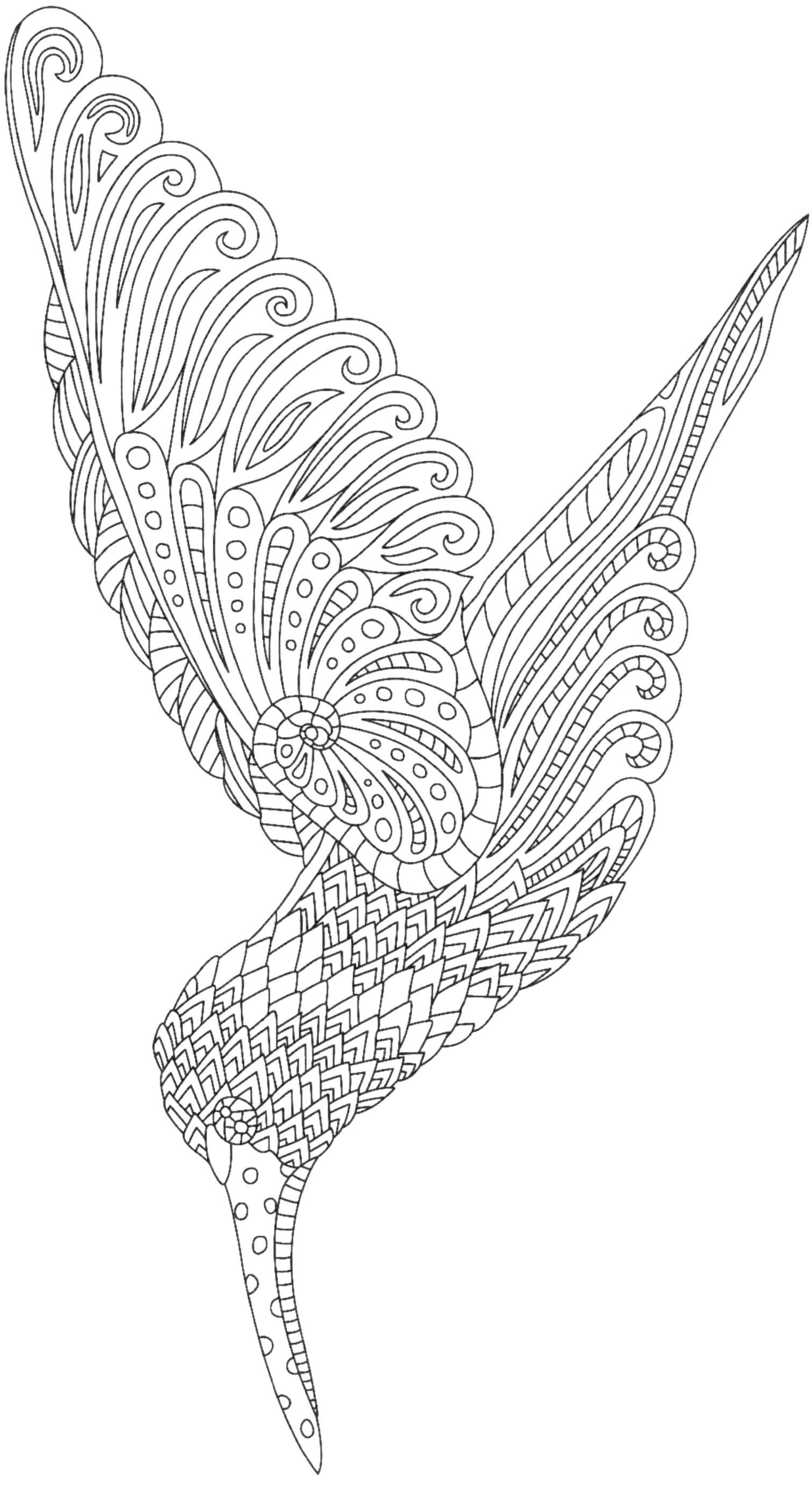

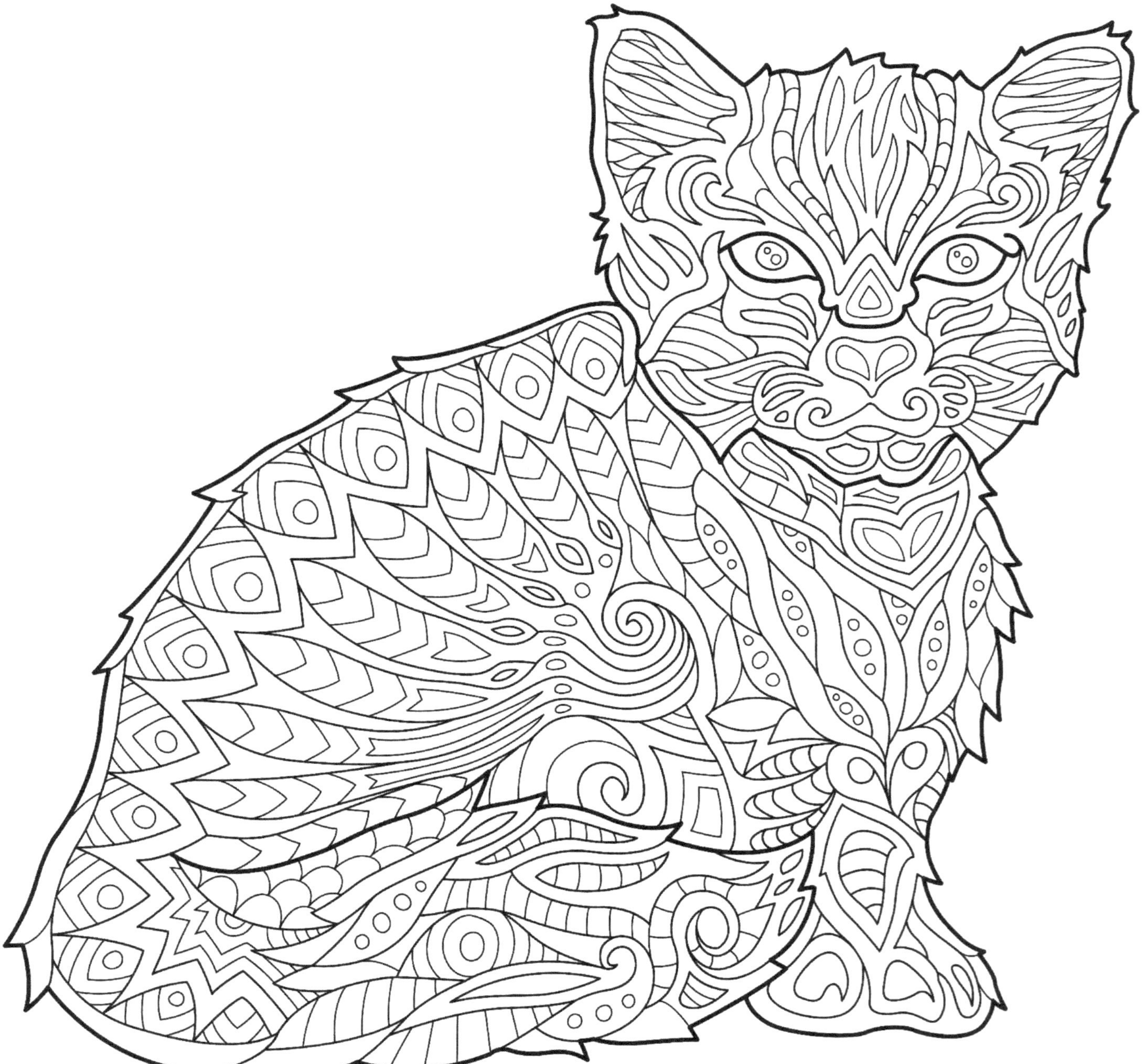

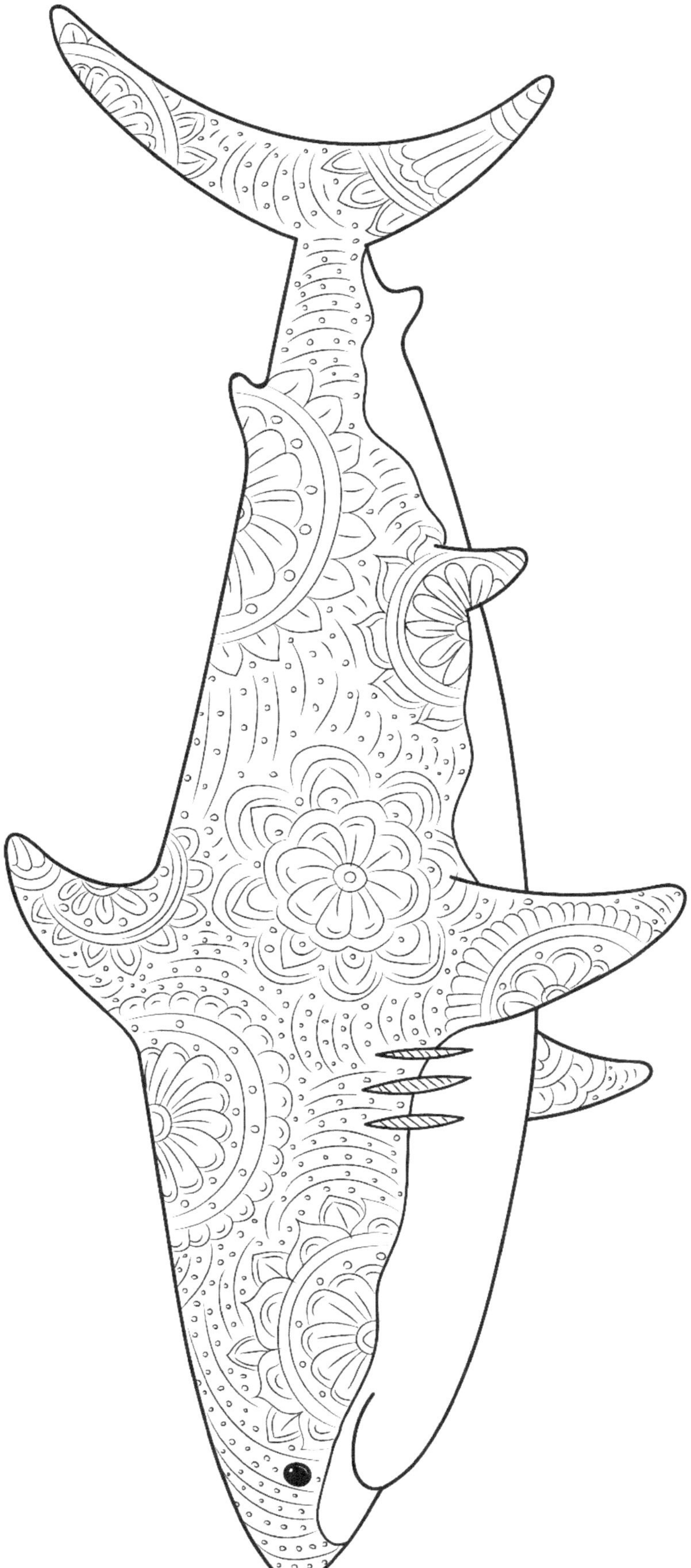

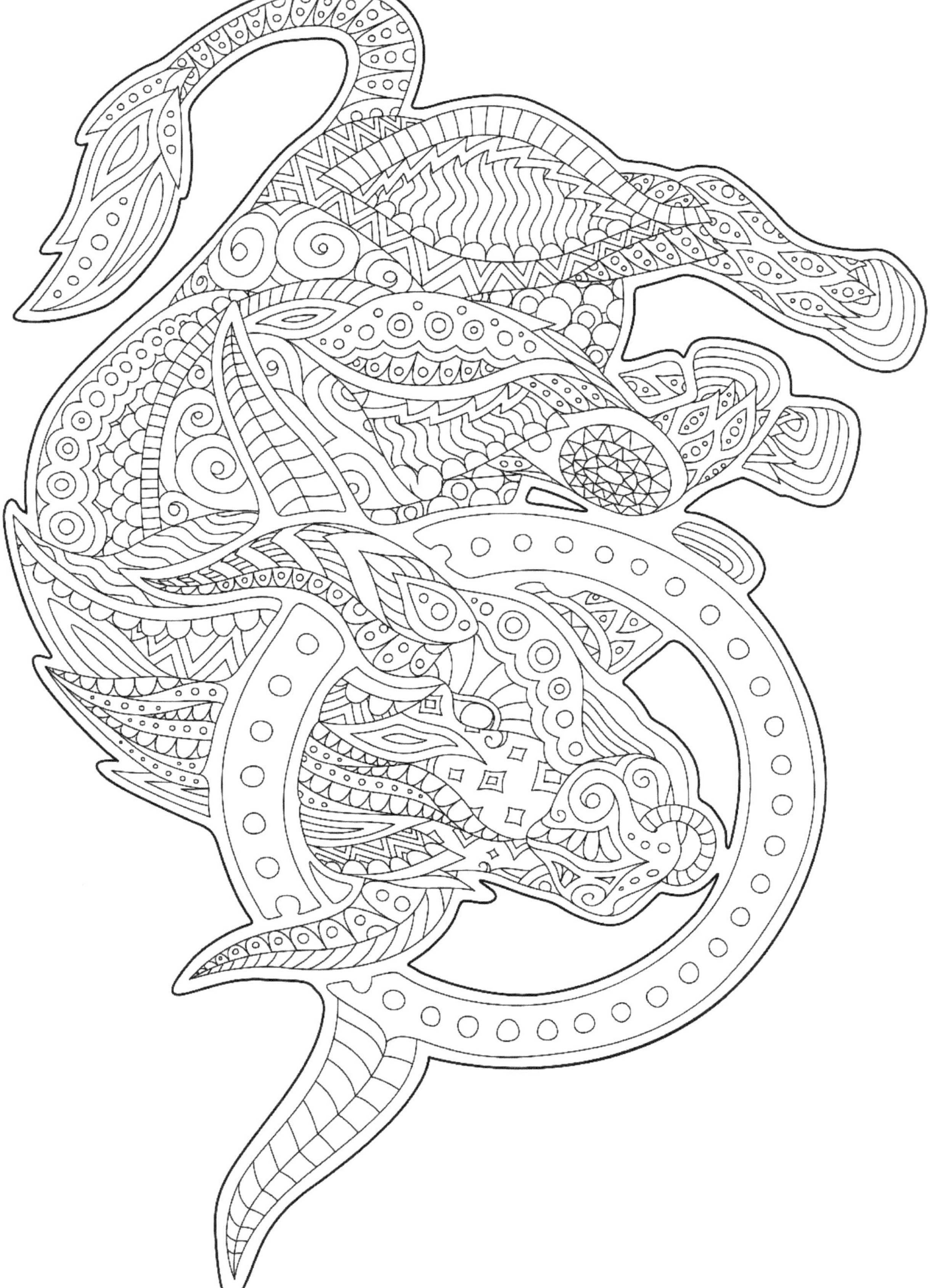

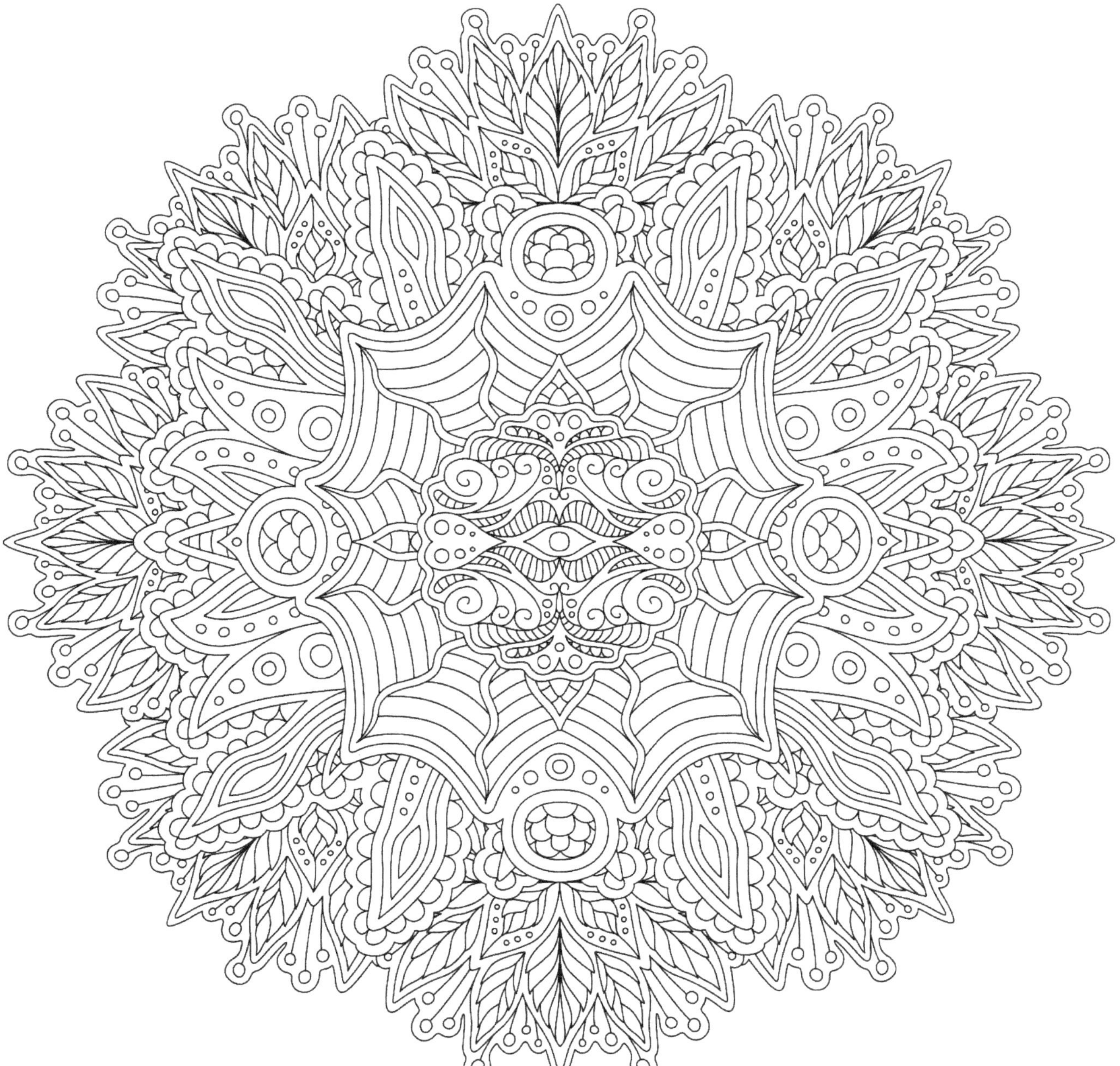

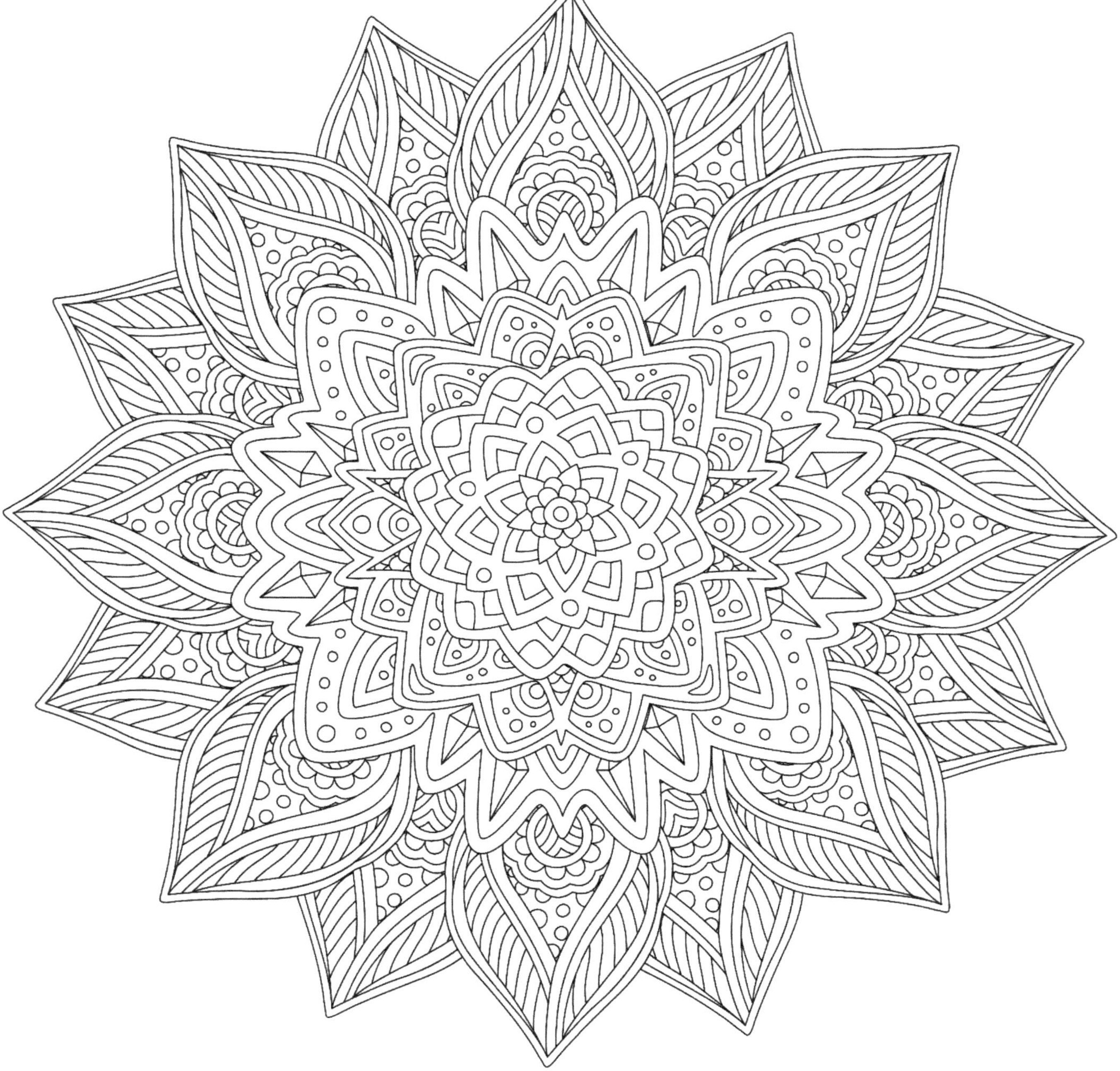

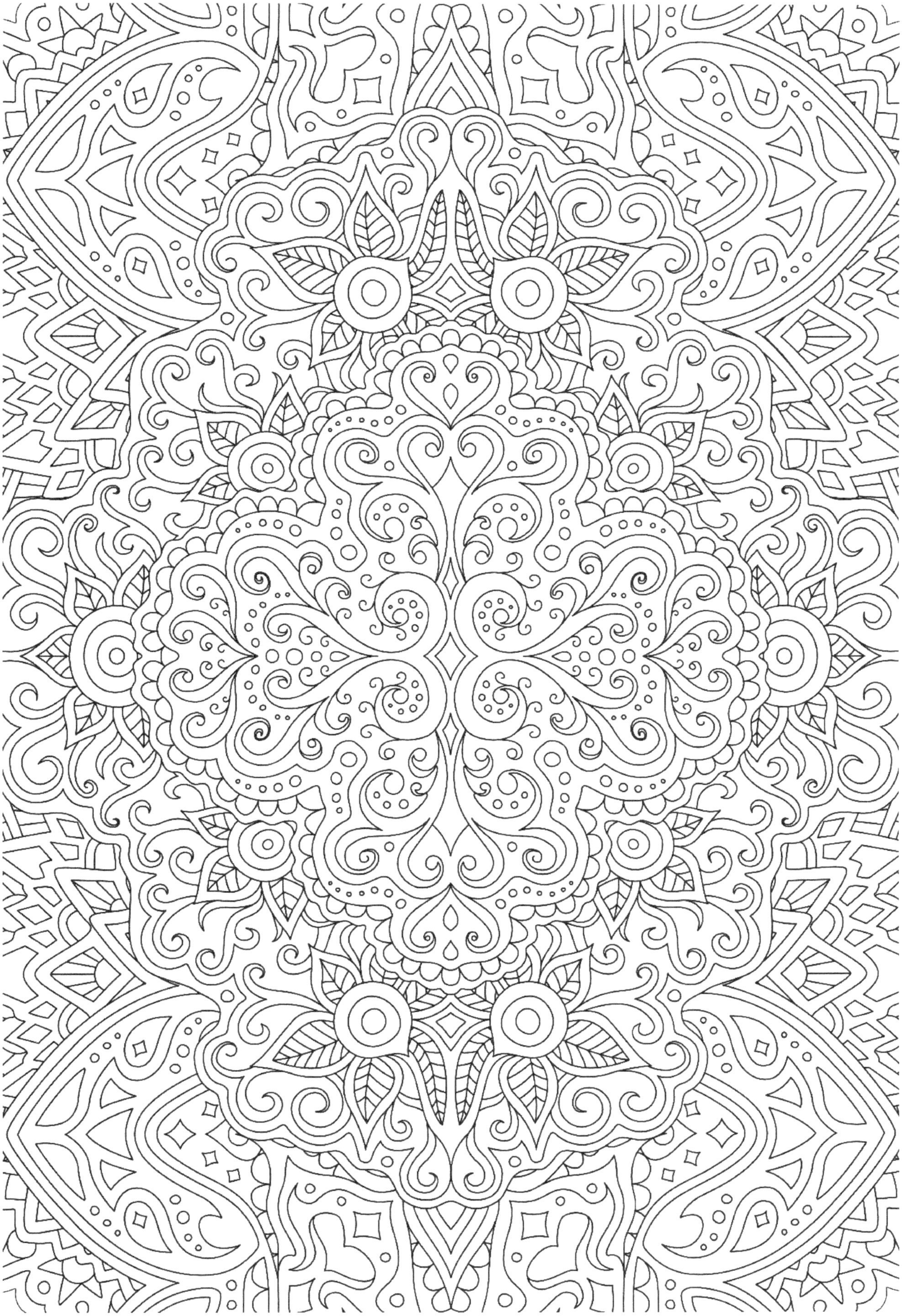

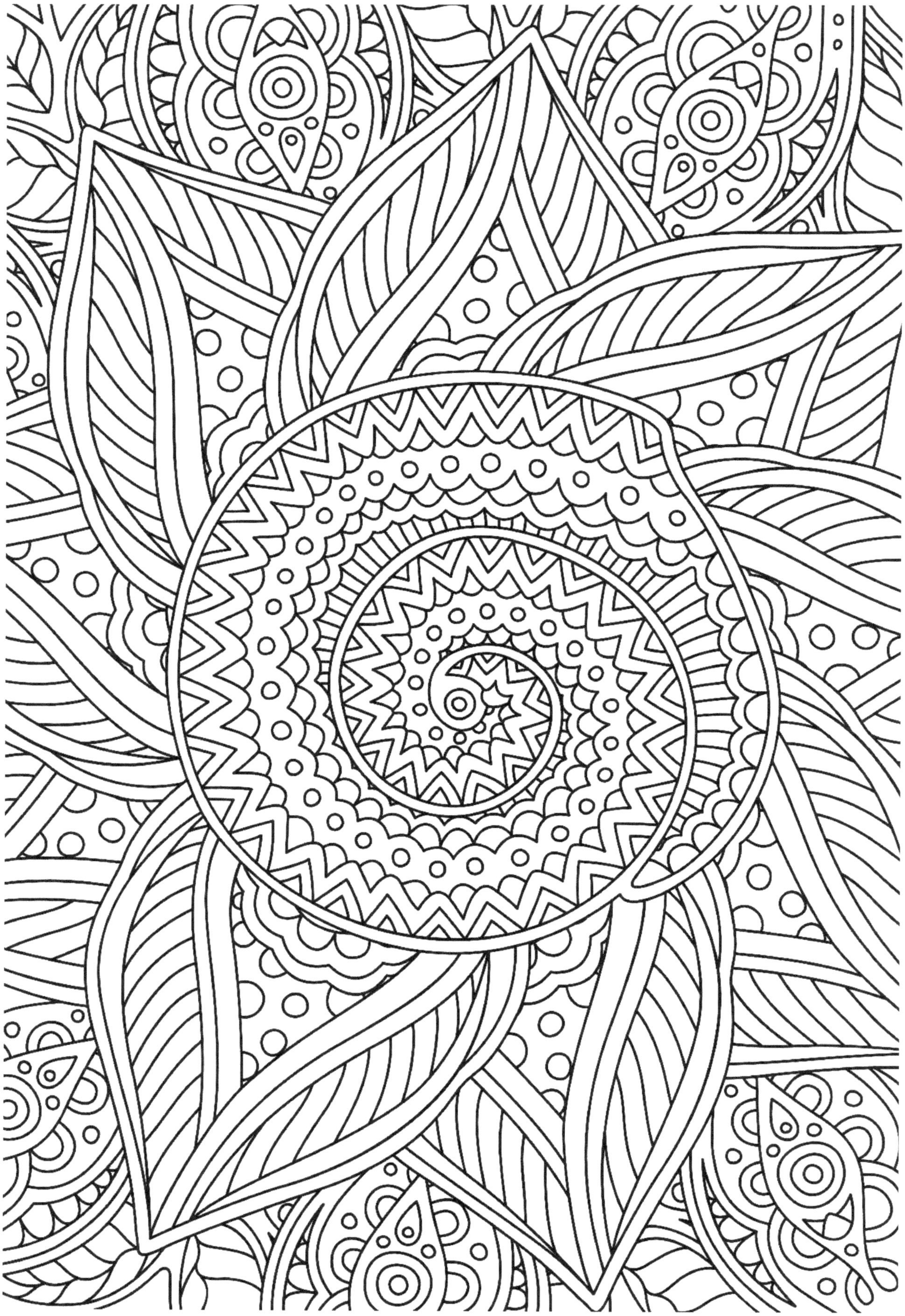

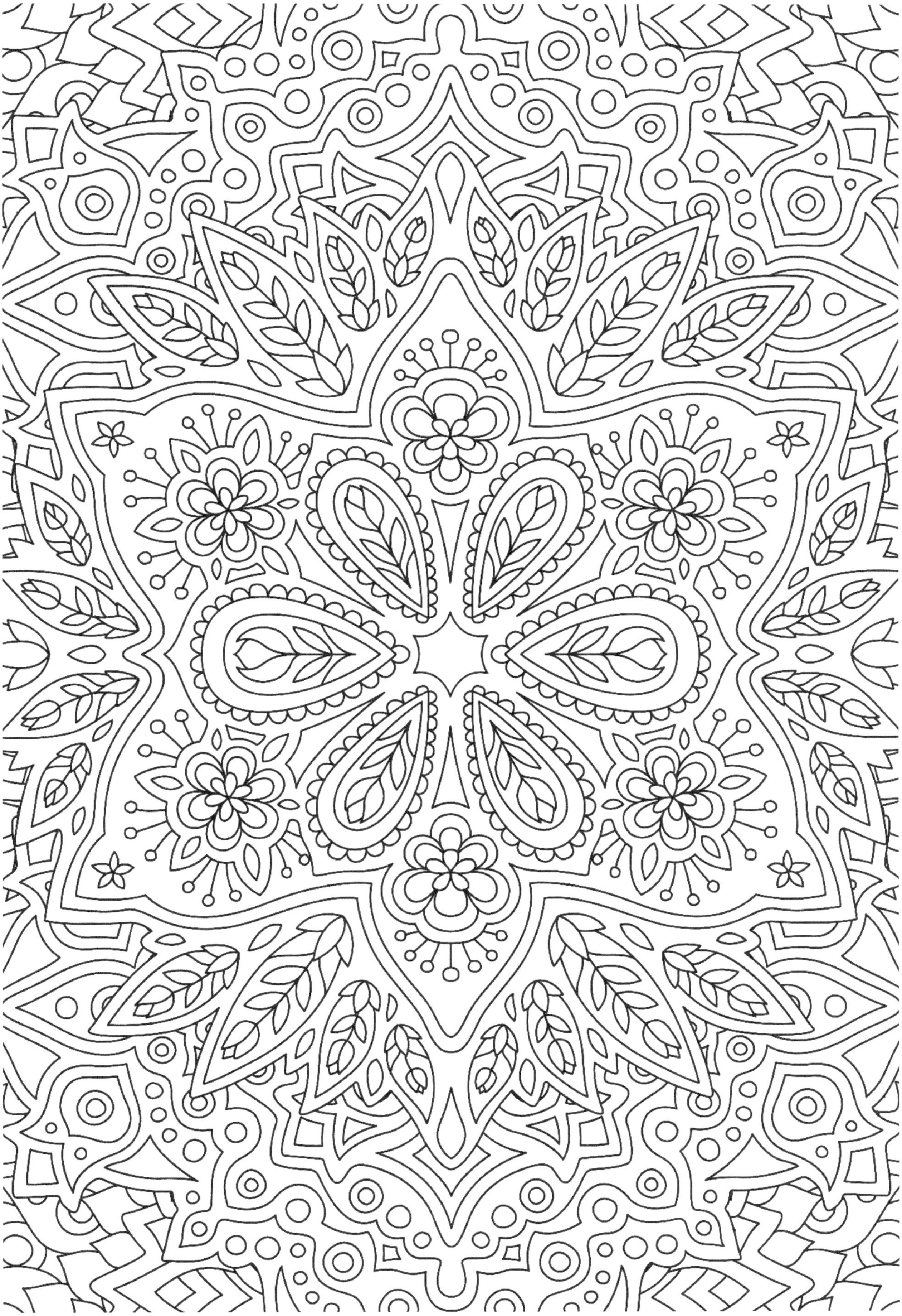

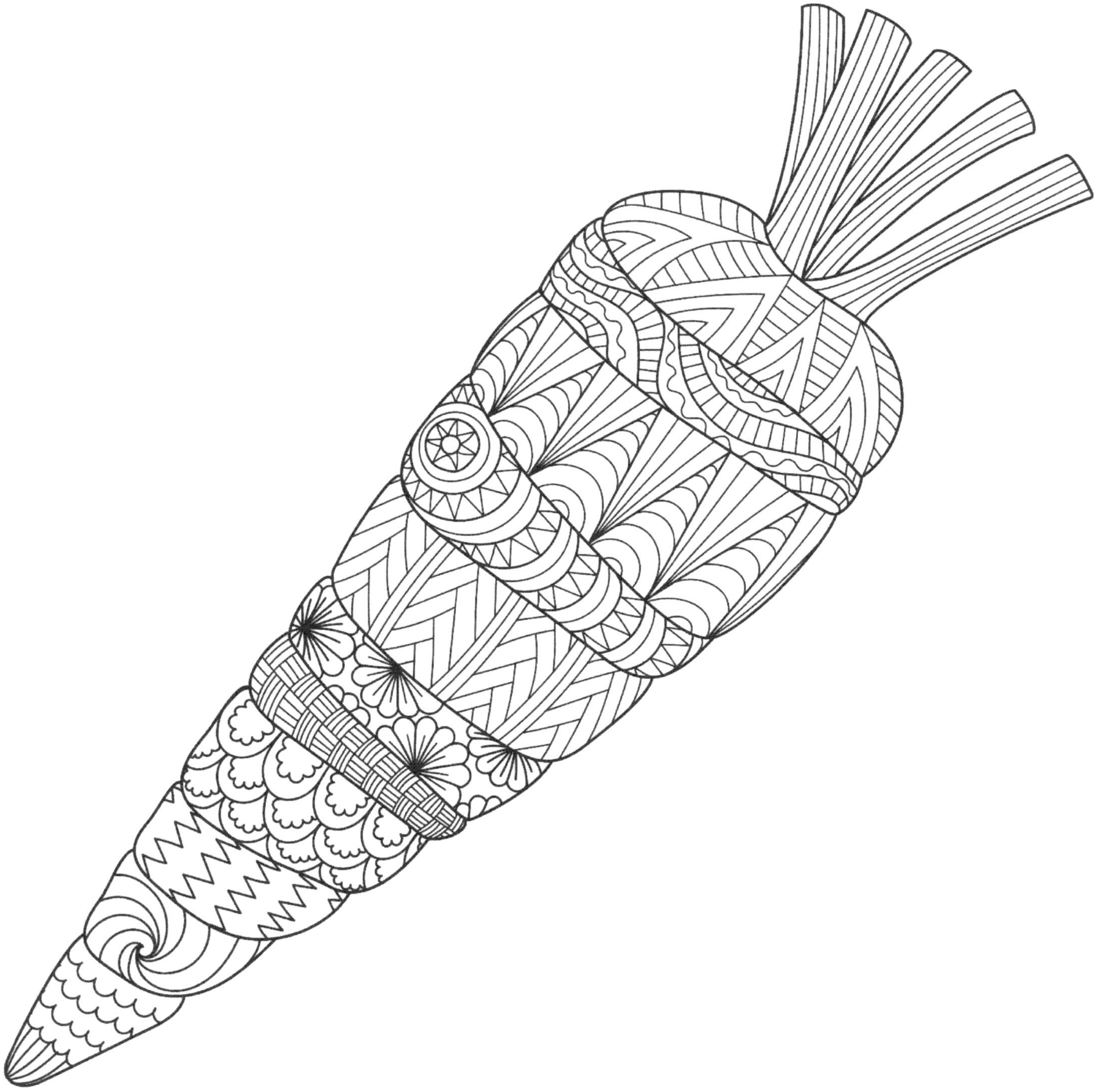

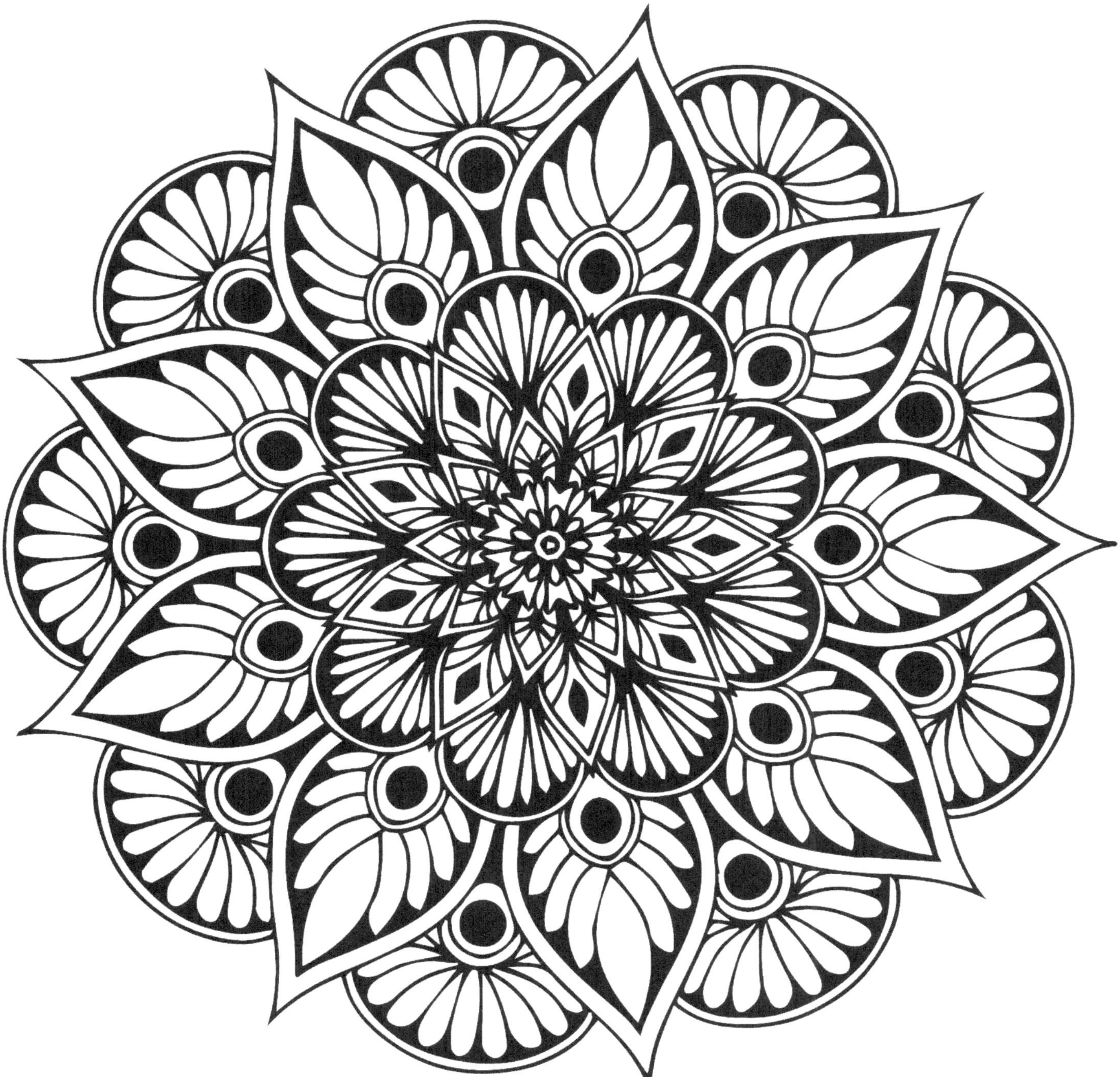

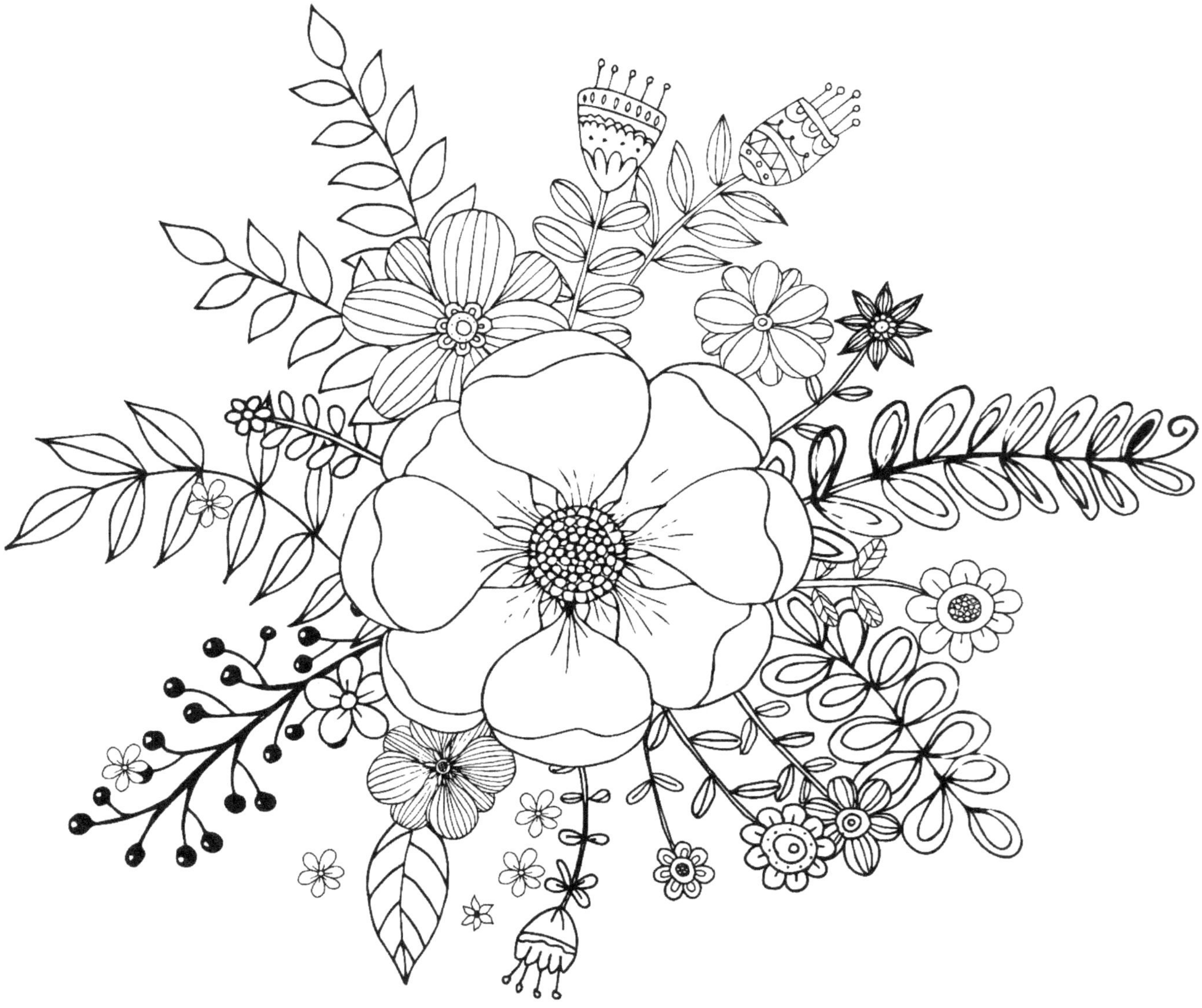

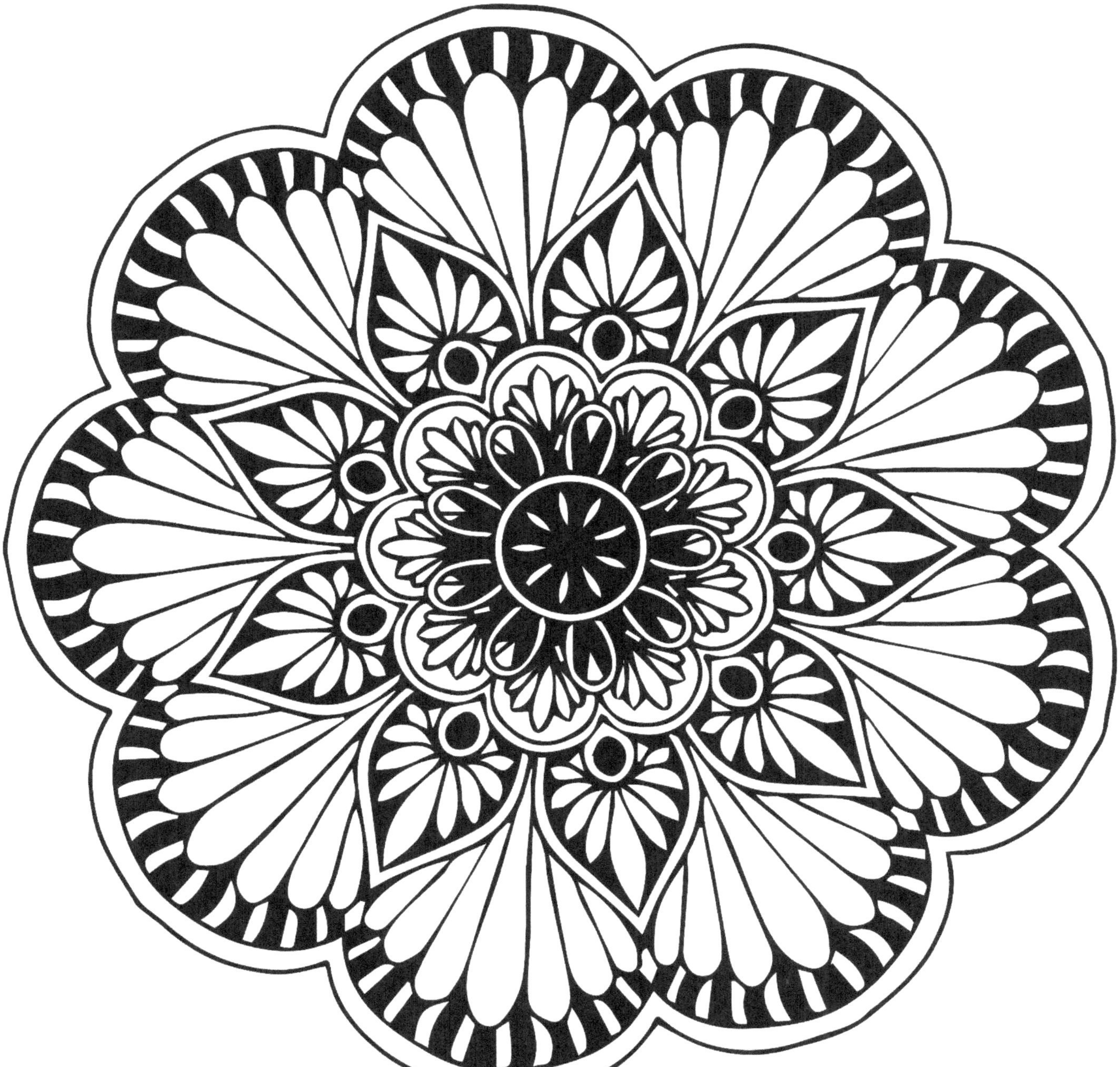

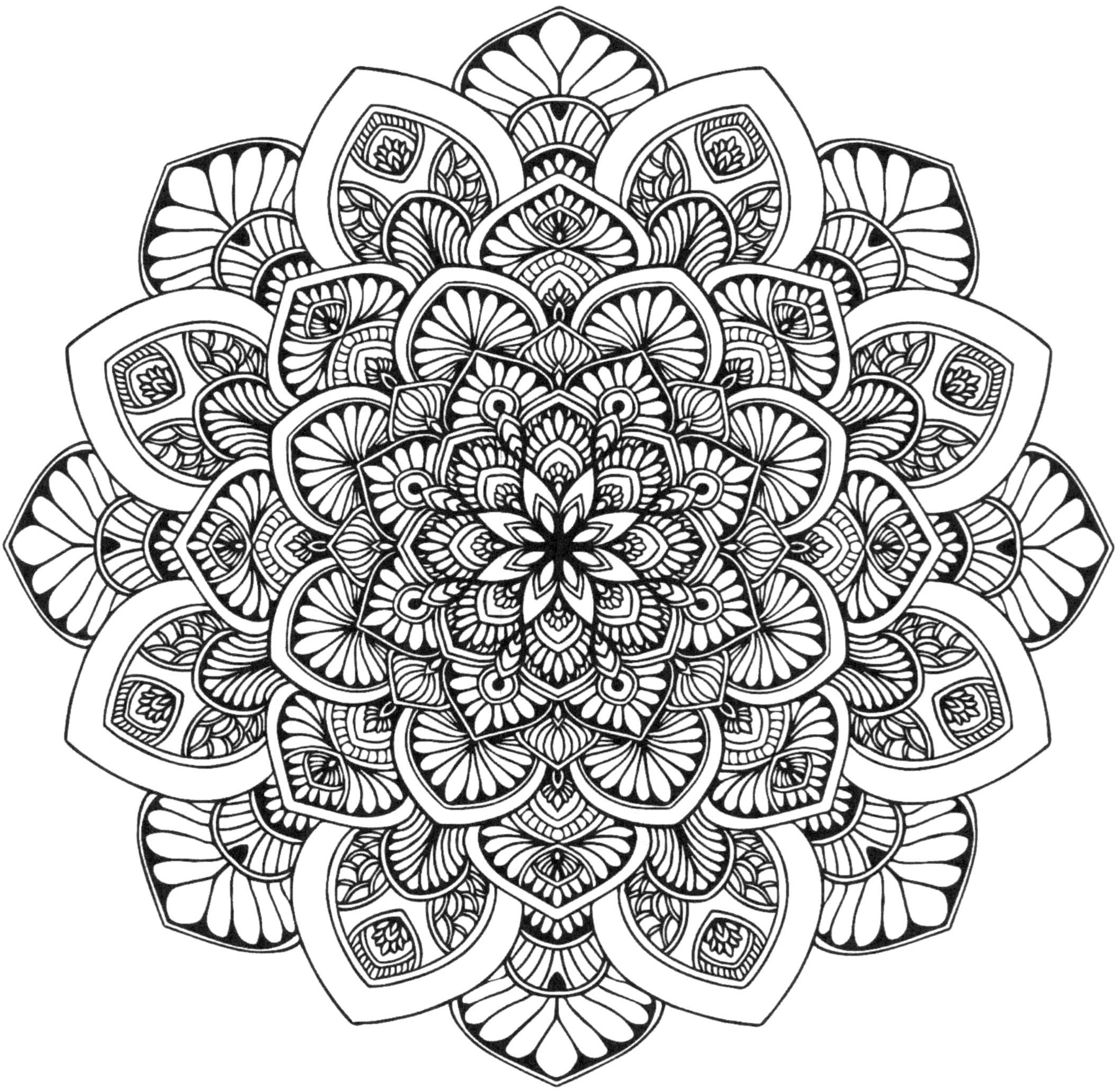

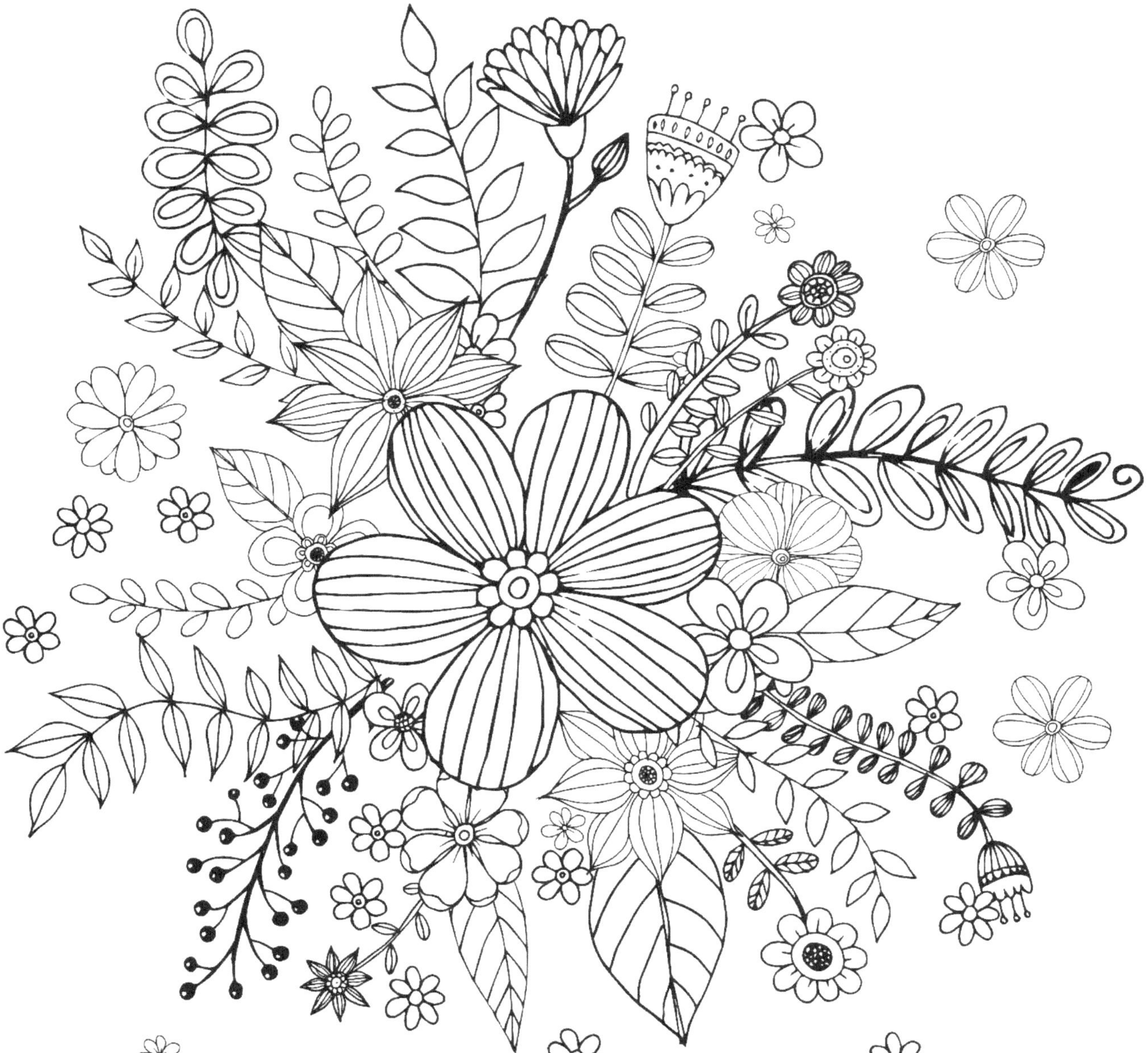

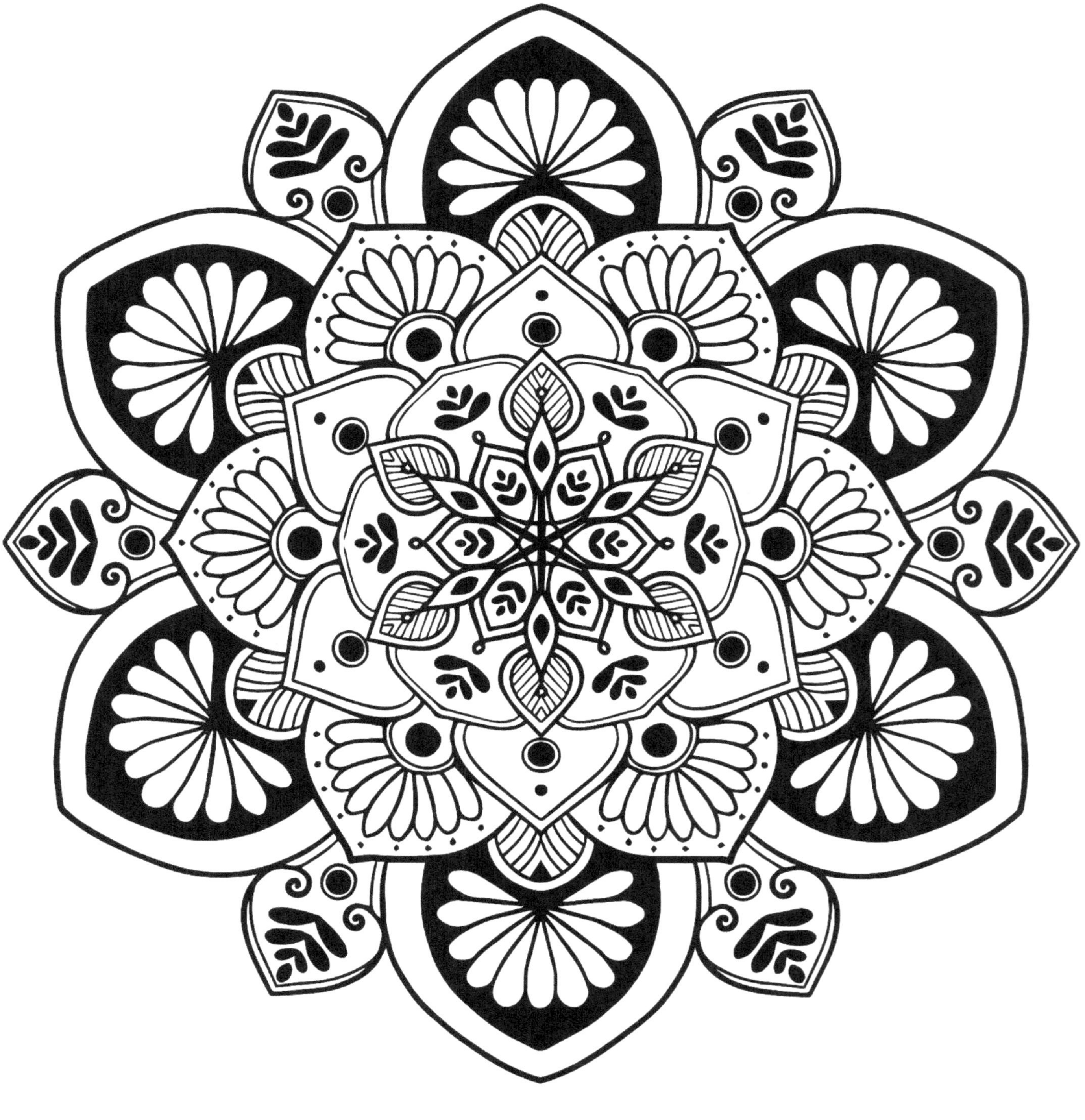

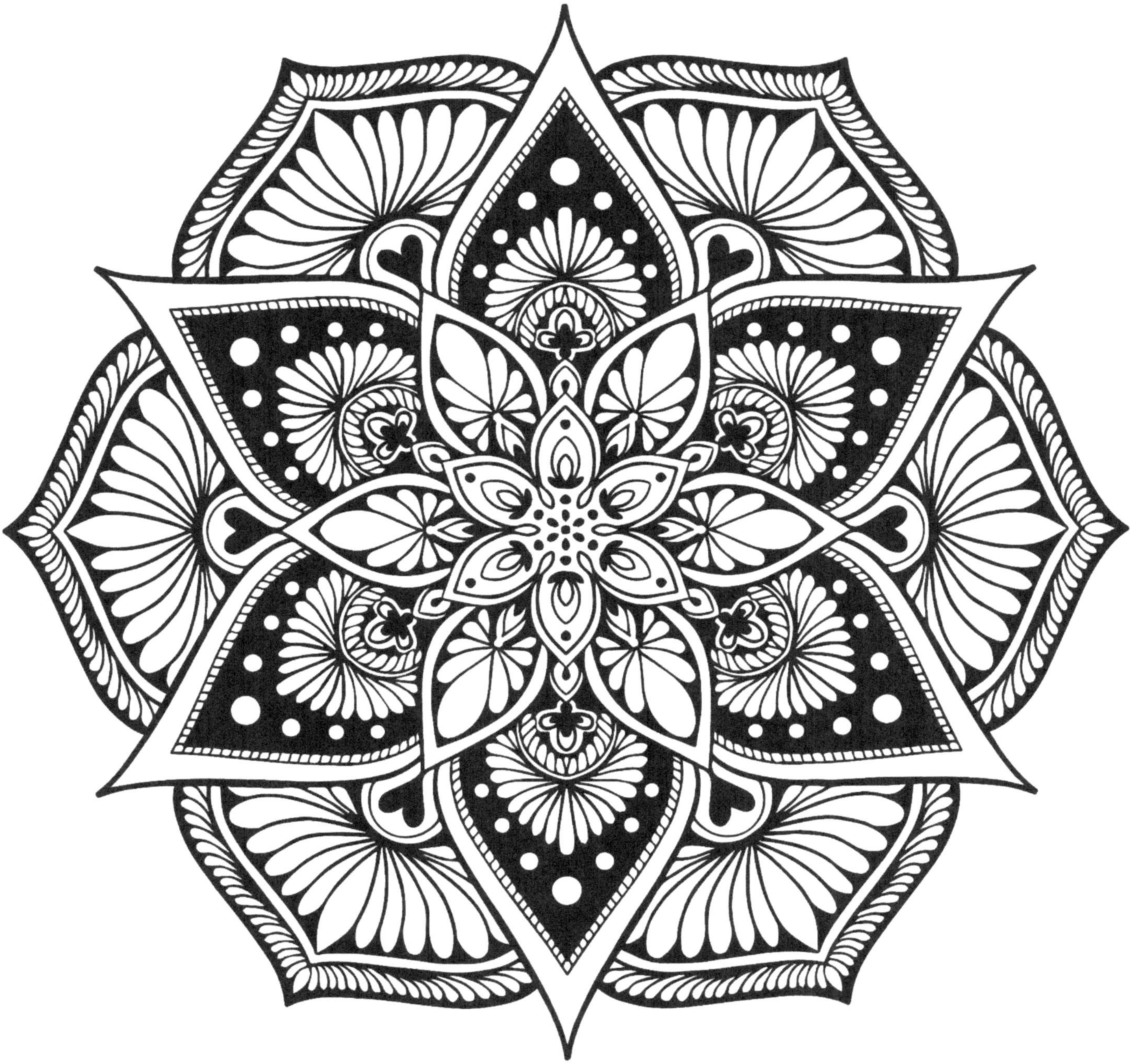

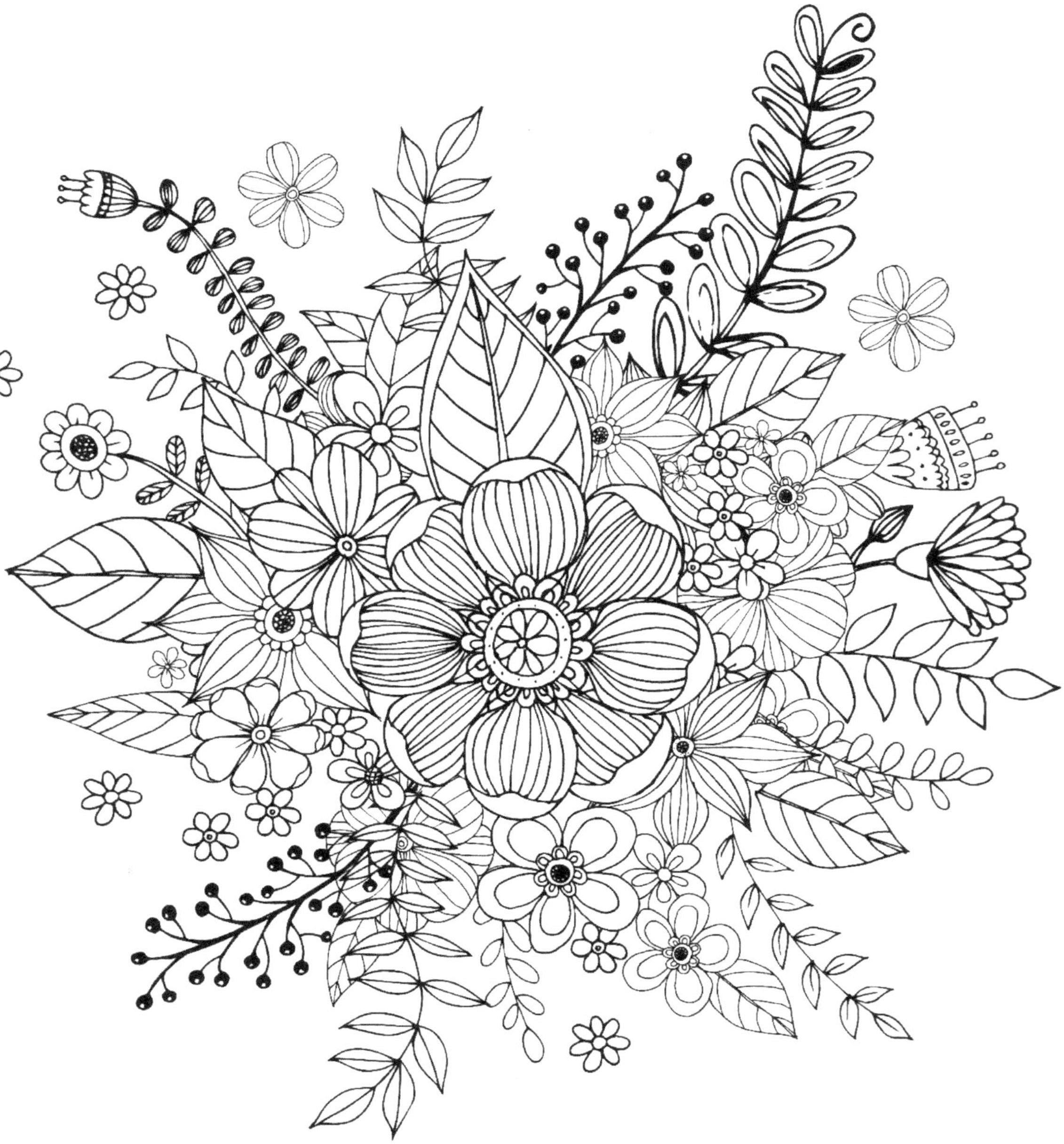

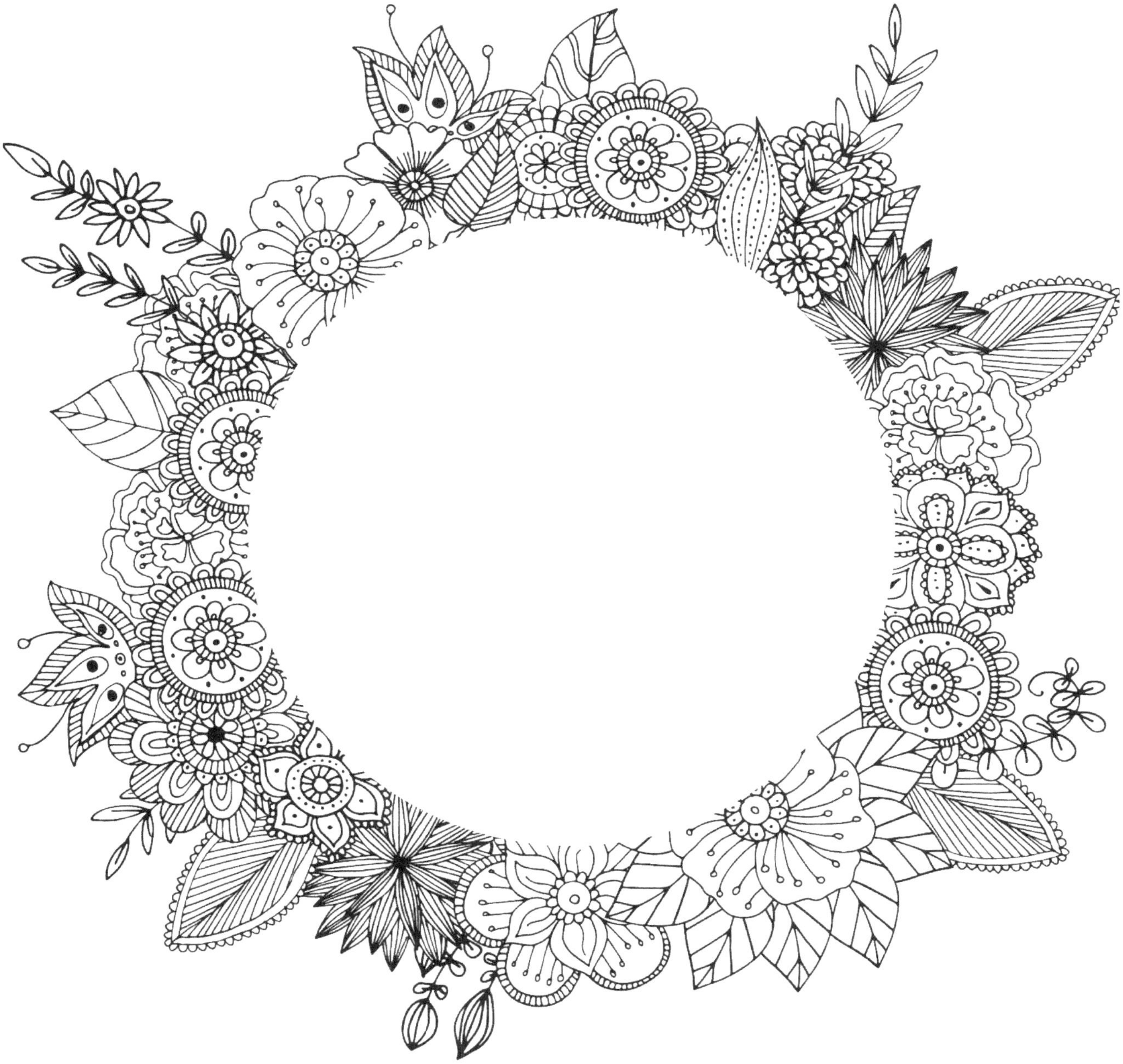

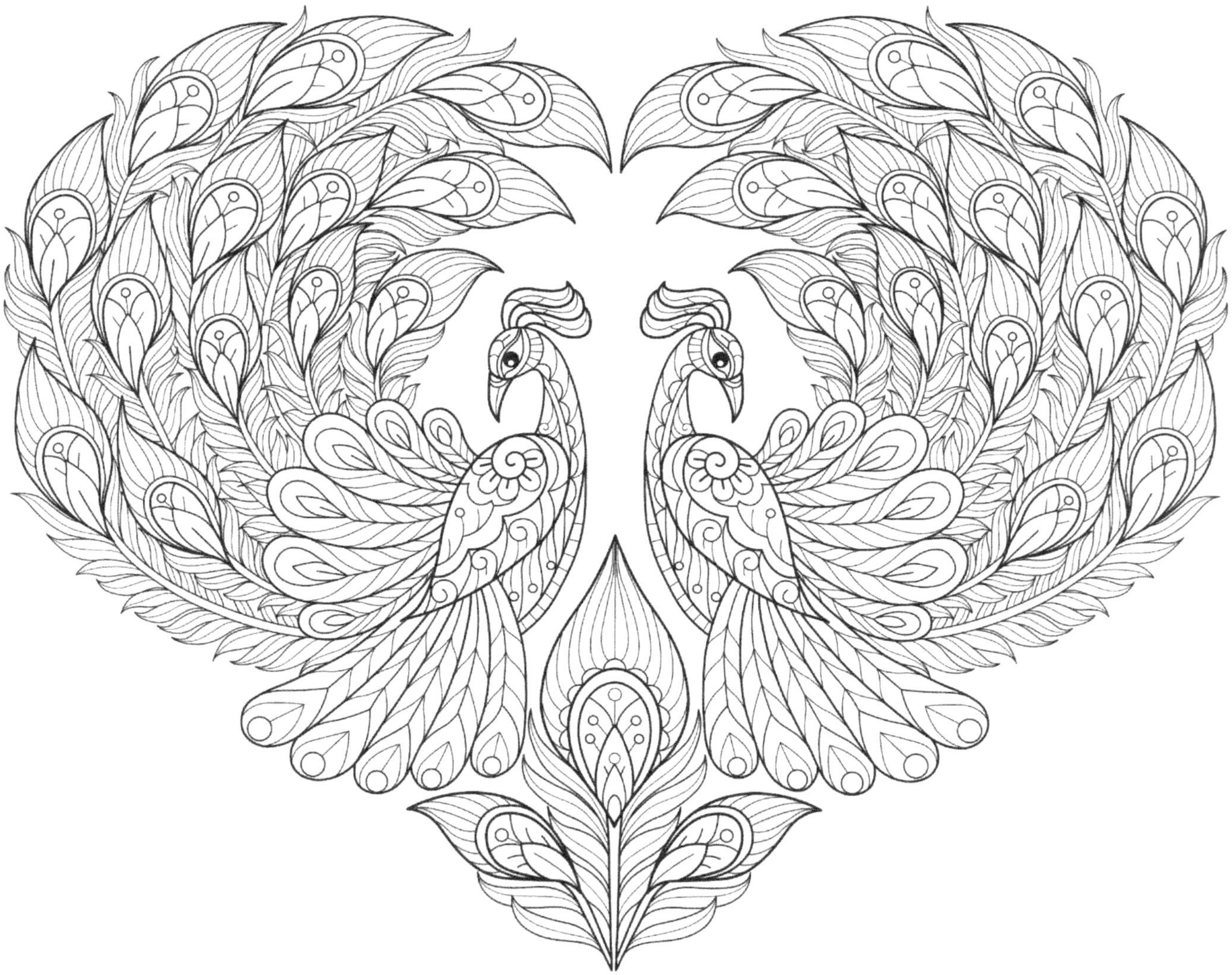

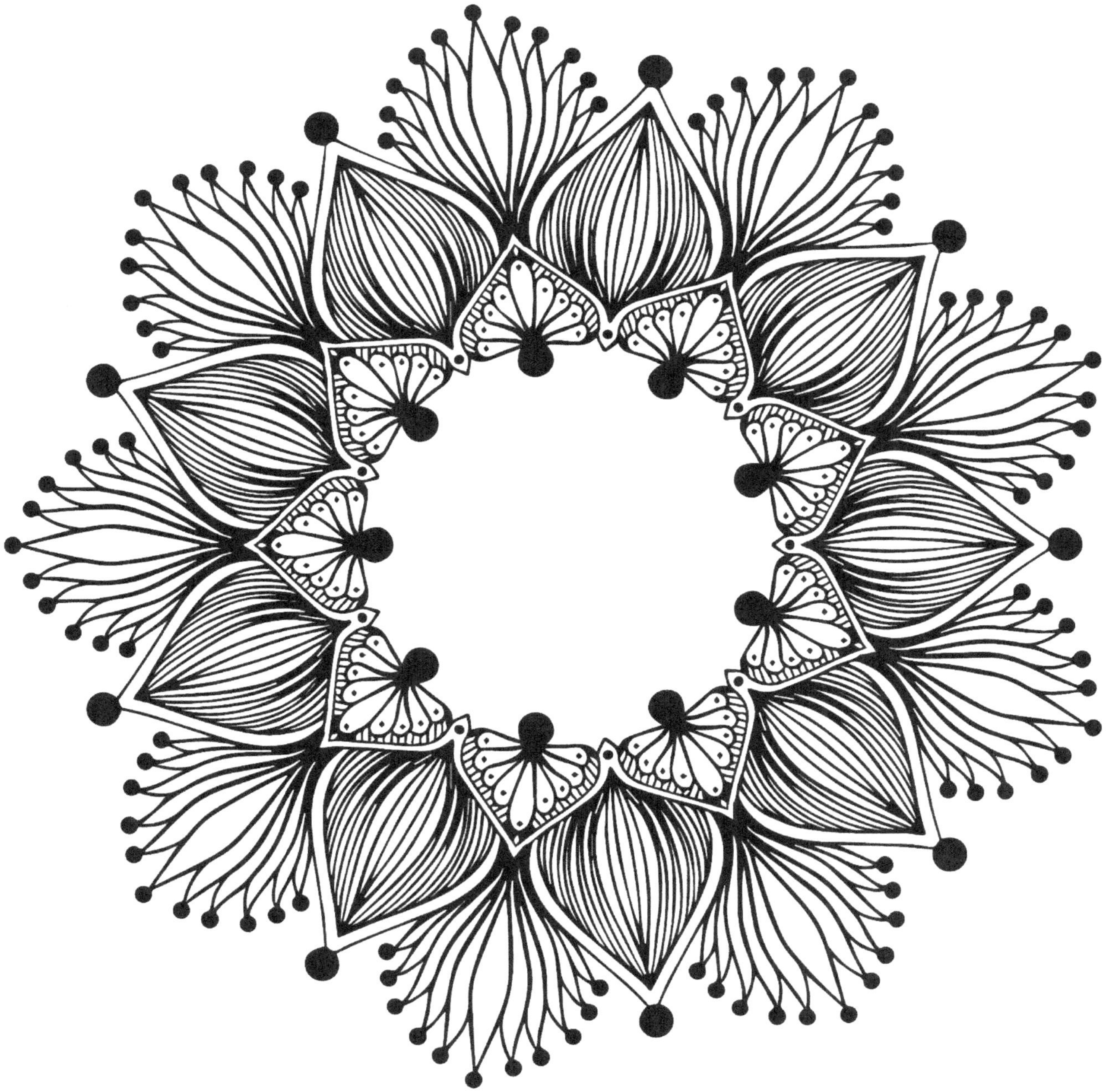

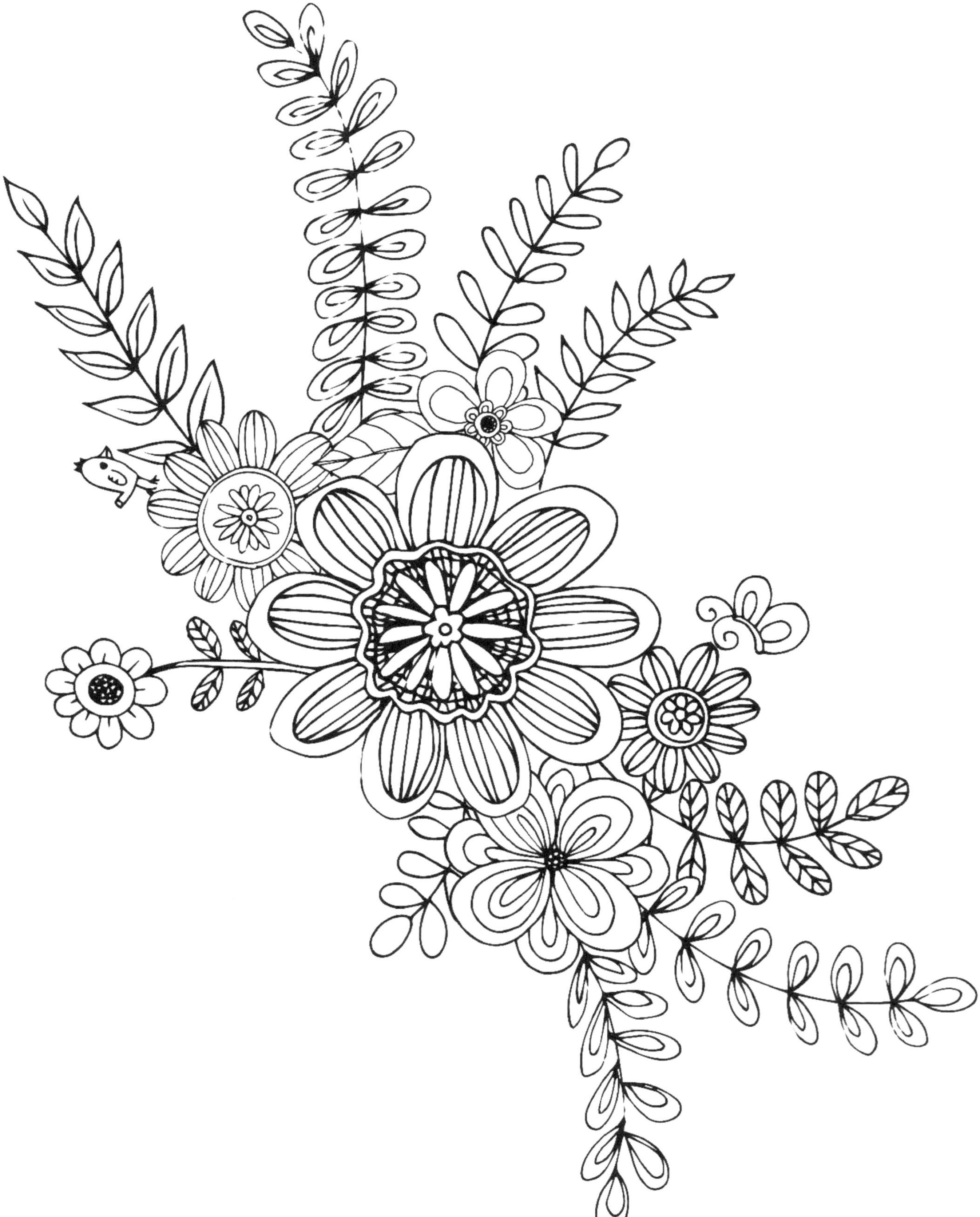

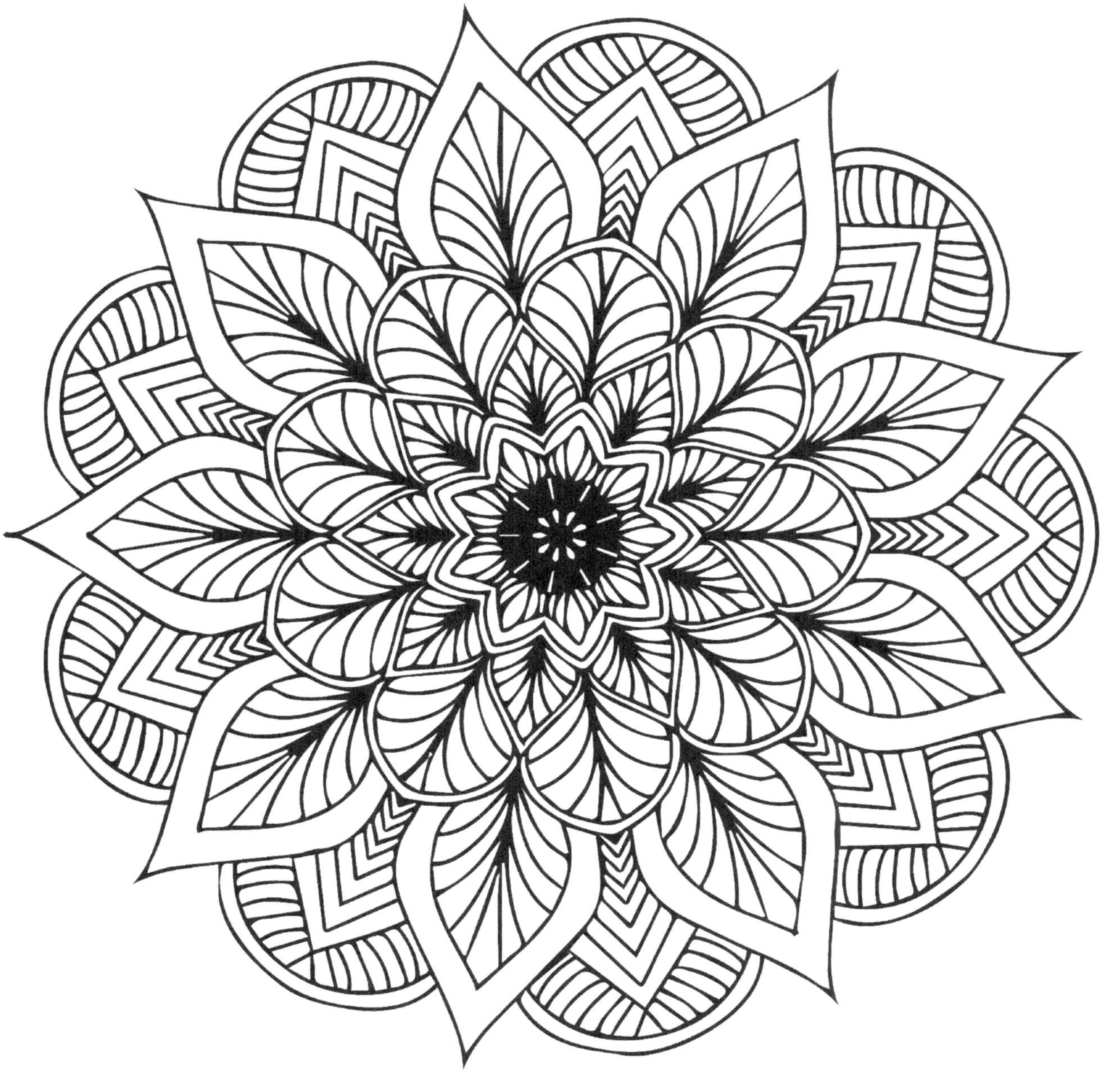

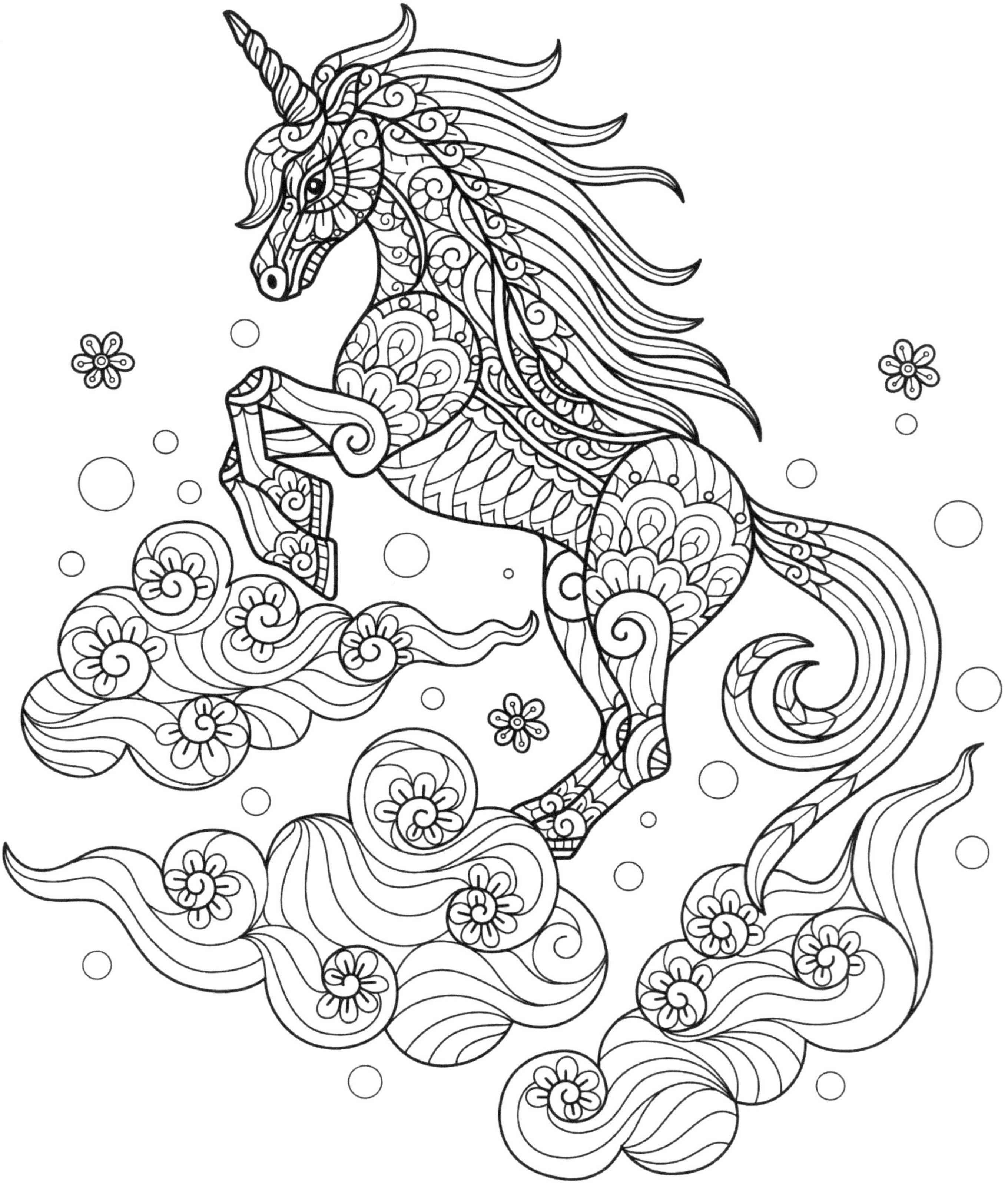

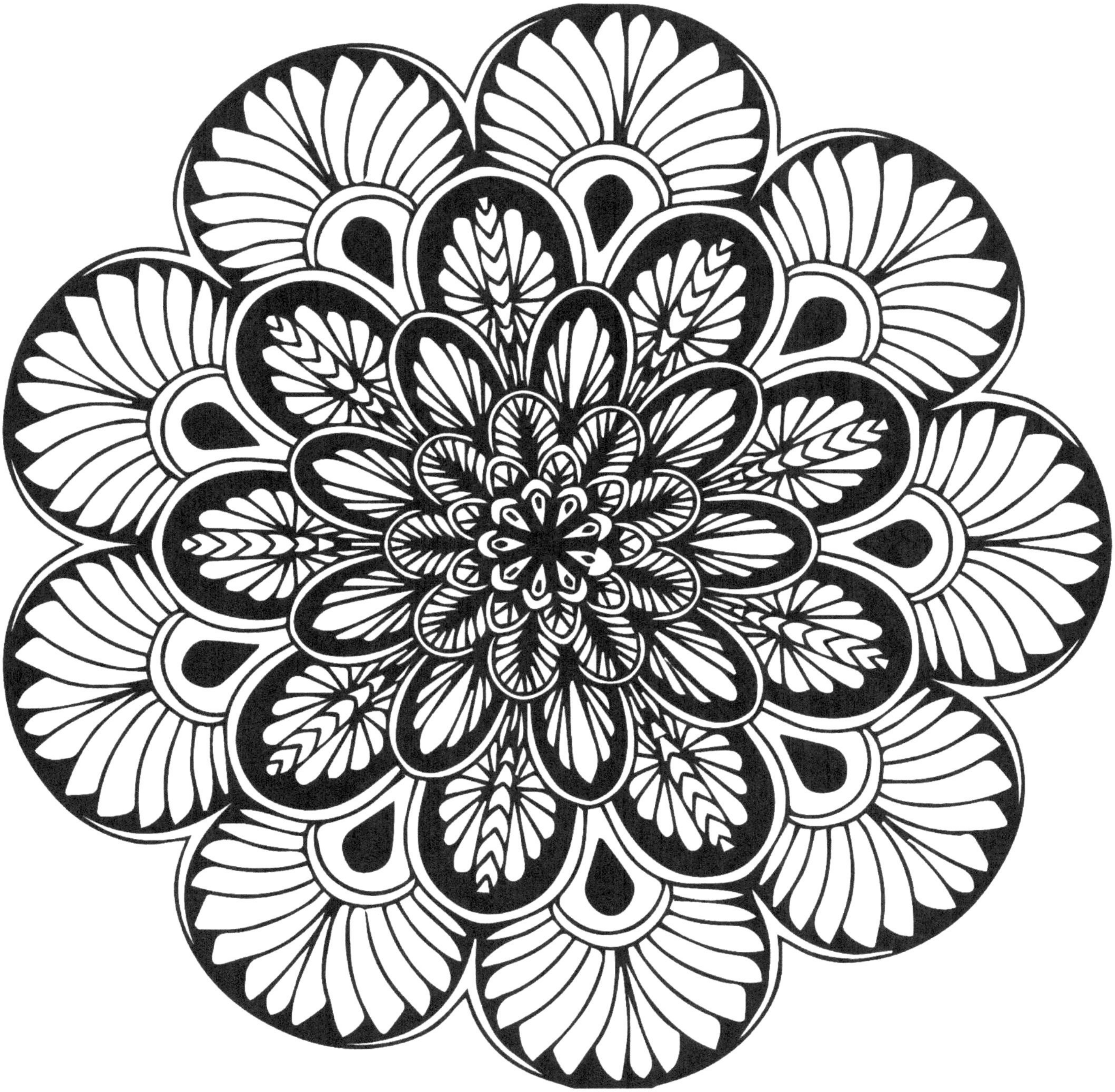

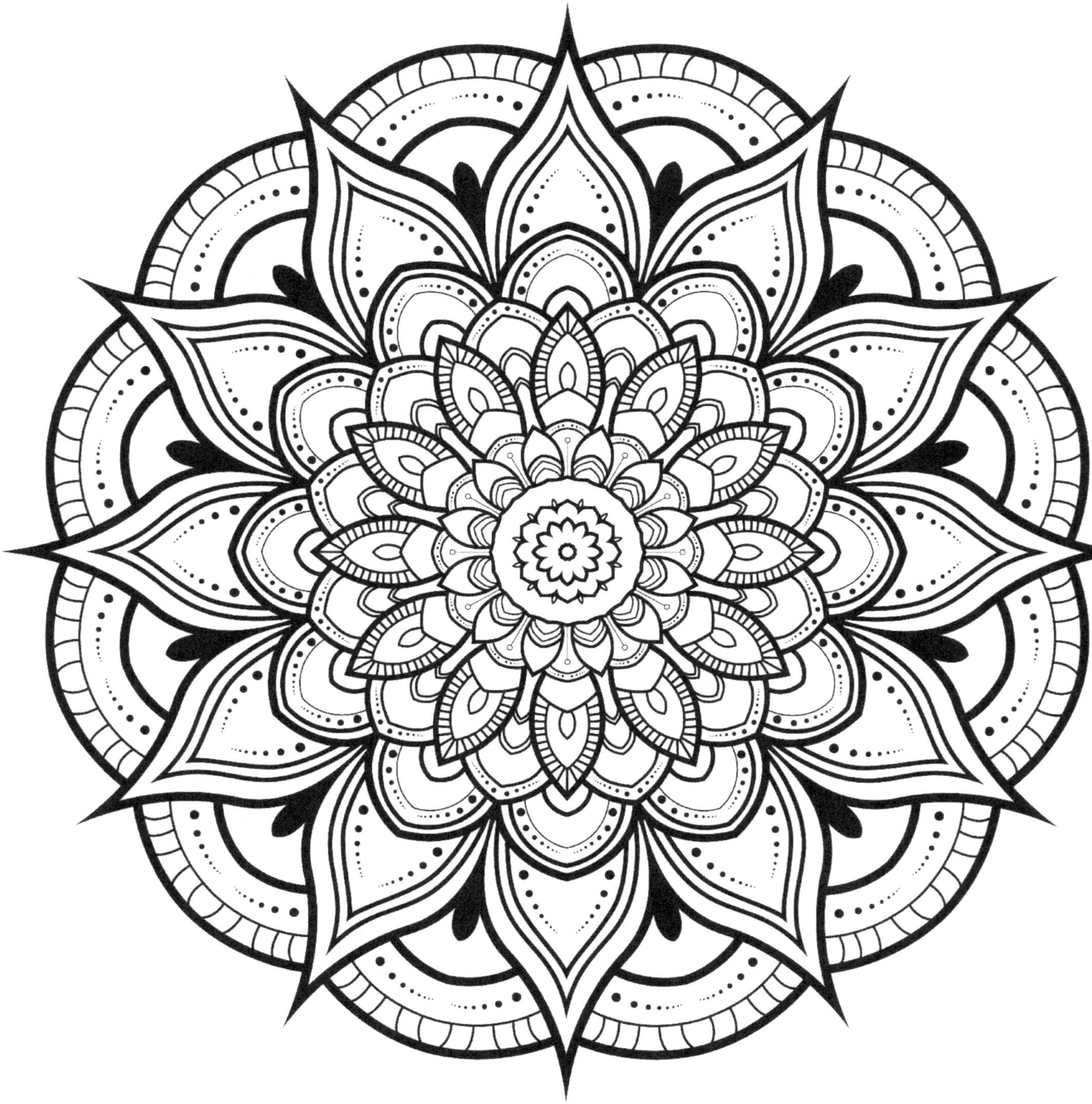

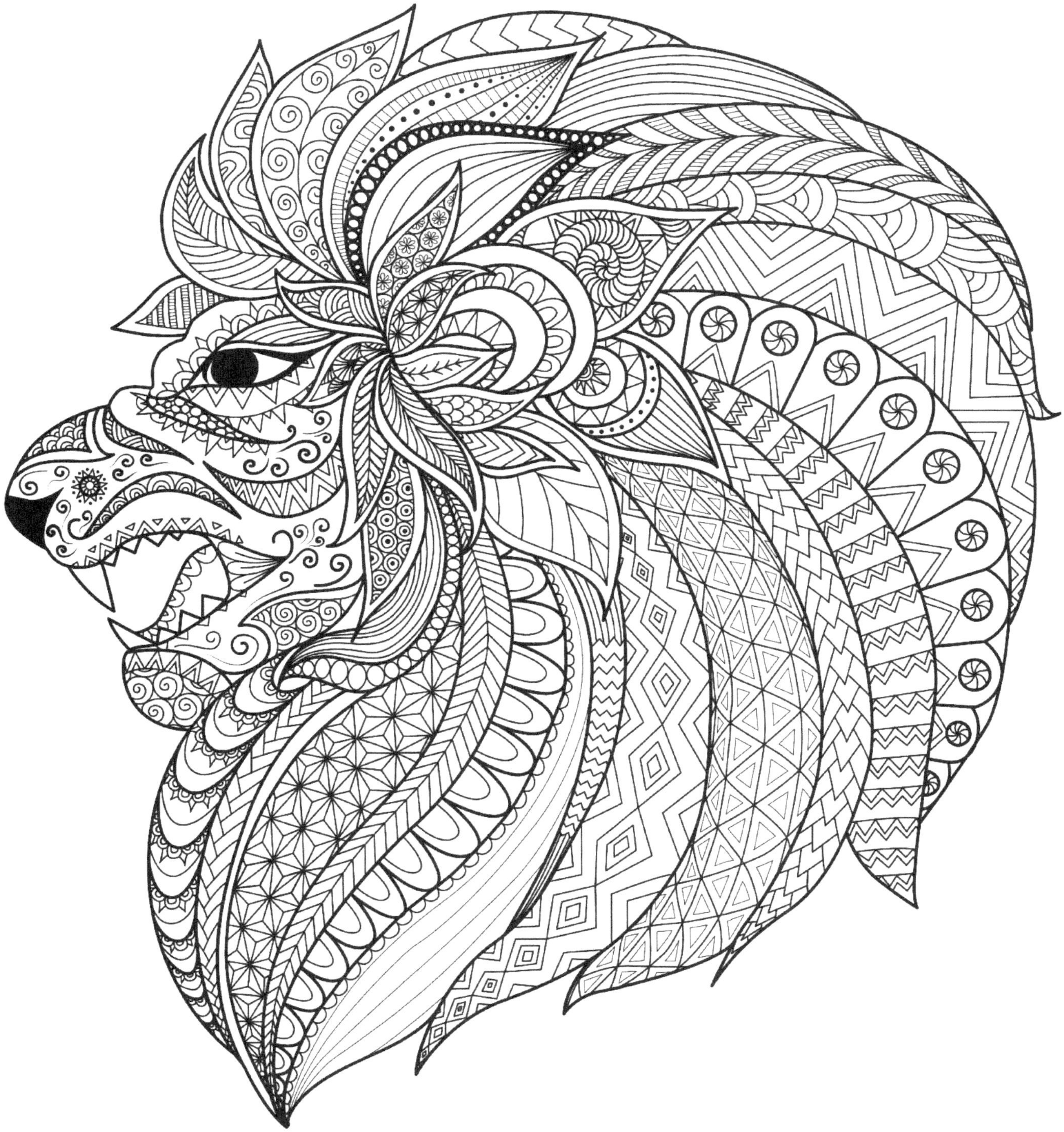

www.ingramcontent.com/pod-product-compliance
Lightning Source LLC
Chambersburg PA
CBHW060438220526
45465CB00008B/3190
9798666797181